# Making the Most of the Cloud

## *How to Choose and Implement the Best Services for Your Library*

### Robin Hastings

THE SCARECROW PRESS, INC.
Lanham • Boulder • New York • Toronto • Plymouth, UK
2014

Published by Scarecrow Press, Inc.
A wholly owned subsidiary of Rowman & Littlefield
4501 Forbes Boulevard, Suite 200, Lanham, Maryland 20706
www.rowman.com

10 Thornbury Road, Plymouth PL6 7PP, United Kingdom

British Library Cataloguing in Publication Information Available

**Library of Congress Cataloging-in-Publication Data**

Hastings, Robin, 1973–
Making the most of the cloud : how to choose and implement the best services for your library / Robin Hastings.
p. cm.
Includes bibliographical references and index.
ISBN 978-0-8108-9109-8 (pbk. : alk. paper) — ISBN 978-0-8108-9110-4 (ebook) 1. Web services—Library applications. 2. Cloud computing. 3. Libraries—Information technology. 4. Electronic information resources—Management. I. Title.
Z674.75.W67H37 2014
006.7'8—dc23
2013027500

Printed in the United States of America

# Contents

# Preface

It seems nearly clichéd to say it, but we are living in exciting times. Cloud-based services are providing more and more functionality that used to be the sole purview of the enterprise-sized business to smaller and smaller organizations. Even the smallest, most rural, or most technologically limited libraries can now have a business-class mail system for little or nothing in the way of financial cost and with a very shallow learning curve—no requirements to host a server or understand the arcane language of SMTP or even know exactly how to register a domain name; cloud-based e-mail services can do all of that for you for free or very, very cheaply. No library needs to go without professional-level graphics or enterprise-class backups or even a world-class Integrated Library System (ILS)—even if they have nothing more than a couple of not-so-new desktop machines with which to work. Cloud services are leveling the playing field in technology in astonishing ways—and we are at the cusp of seeing those benefits accrue to our organizations.

While there is some disagreement on the exact nature of the "cloud" (see the first chapter of this book for a discussion on the definition[s] of "cloud" in the technological sense), the fact is that you can barely go anywhere without seeing advertisements for cloud services and cloud-based software offerings and cloud-management functions all around you. Whatever the definition you prefer, the fact is that ignoring the "cloud" is not really possible any longer.

Another "feature" of the cloud being so new is a definite instability in the cloud-based services landscape. Just as this book was being finished, a major Database as a Service (DaaS) provider went out of business with a two-week notice for those who were paying for the service and a one-week notice for those using the free version. This means that organizations that were relying on this company to provide them with cloud-hosted database services are scrambling to find new cloud providers (see chapter 6, "Software as a Service (SaaS)," for more discussion of this very situation). Knowing what to look for to try to avoid this scenario happening to you and how to react if and when it does is vital. Sometimes you will pick a solid-looking vendor who has been in business for a while and seems like they'll be in business for a while longer and they will turn around and disappear on you—sometimes without even a week's notice. This is becoming a more common event and knowing how to evaluate and then respond when things like this happen could be the difference between you having access to a critical bit of your organization or not having access. This book will help you as you come across these and other, less serious issues in the cloud.

Since cloud services are so new, there are a number of issues with procuring them for any organization. Libraries are no different in that they need to be able to compare and contrast services that may seem to be apples and oranges in order to find the service that works for their particular needs. No one cloud service will work for every library, just like no one ILS has worked for all libraries. This book begins by defining then making the case for cloud-based services in your library.

I wrote *Making the Most of the Cloud: How to Choose and Implement the Best Services for Your Library* to assist the nontechnical librarian in finding, evaluating, and procuring a cloud service or services that will work for his or her library. It will also be valuable even for technical librarians who just want some insight into what sort of things to be thinking of when researching cloud-based services for their libraries. I profile a number of different services—from the ILS in the cloud to web hosting and backups to the sort of thing that has traditionally been managed with software: project management and graphical editing. I also profile general software (as a service), as well as computer management from the cloud and social media management from the cloud. Security and training services and issues finish the discussion of cloud-based functionality. I research, evaluate, and present all of these various things—things libraries already deal with in traditional ways—in this book. Of course, things change—software providers come and go—so general principles of what sort of things librarians should look for in a cloud provider are included in each chapter. This will make the book useful even when the landscape has changed and many of the providers that are so entrenched today become obsolete and/or dead.

Things change, even more so in the realm of technology, so the afterword (chapter 14), which includes lists of resources, will be supplemented by a regularly checked and updated web page. See http://www.rhastings.net/cloudbook/resources for new graphical software and security resources. This site will be updated and revised for the next few years to come, at least, in support of this book.

Overall, the outlook for cloud-based computing is rosy. You will be in the position of deciding whether to use a cloud vendor or cloud-based service in the not-so-distant future, if you haven't already. *Making the Most of the Cloud: How to Choose and Implement the Best Services for Your Library* will give you the tools you need to make those decisions and consider those risks in a clearheaded and informed way. Hopefully, by the time you have read this book, you will have an understanding of what services are, and are not, viable for your organization. You will have the ability to evaluate and decide which service to use and the confidence to put your chosen solution in place for your organization. Most of you will have a perfectly smooth experience with your cloud ventures—things will work the way they should and you will save time and money in your day-to-day operations. That's the ideal of the cloud and something that, in the future, will be a given. For today, however, read this book, consider critically the claims of your chosen cloud service providers, and watch the cloud-laden future unfold before you.

# Acknowledgments

I'd like to thank Blake Carver for being so cheerfully helpful when I had questions and demands to make of him during the writing of this book—it was much appreciated. I'd also like to thank my parents for being so very supportive and my son, Alex, for being so very undemanding of me while I concentrated on my writing. Last, but certainly not least, I want to acknowledge the great help Mickey Coalwell provided in indexing this book—it was amazingly kind and very much appreciated. Thanks to you all!!

*Chapter One*

# Definitions and Limits of Cloud Computing

Today, libraries have many options when it comes to how they manage their information technology (IT) resources. In-house is the standard, traditional way to manage servers, networks, and computers. This sort of management requires some expensive staff knowledge and dedicated resources that are becoming, in this day and age, difficult to maintain. Moving IT resources and services to the Internet—using "the cloud"—is one way to help get some economies of scale as well as outside brainpower involved in library technology. As more and more services move to Internet-based offerings, libraries will need to know just what it is they are getting into and how to evaluate and acquire those Internet-based resources in "the cloud."

To give us a standard jumping-off point, a definition that we can all agree on, I'll be using the NIST (National Institute of Standards and Technology) definition of the cloud. They define the cloud as a model of technology that enables constant, convenient, on-demand access to a shared pool of computing resources that can be configured as needed and that can be rapidly built up and released with no more than a little bit of management effort or interaction from the service provider. This definition—as well as more explanation—can be found in the NIST Special Publication 800-145 at http://csrc.nist.gov/publications/nistpubs/800-145/SP800-145.pdf in PDF format.

To be a "cloud" provider, then, the vendor or network provider must be able to provide services when the customer wants them, even if the vendor is not open for business 24/7 (meaning there is no human interaction required on the vendor's part), and those services must be completely configurable and accessible by the customer in a convenient and always-on sort of way. Using this definition, social networking sites like Facebook are clearly cloud services—they allow the customer to create and build out a page (account) with no interaction from the folks at Facebook required and they are always on, pretty easy to use (convenient), and customizable (to an extent, at least) by the customer. They also provide shared network resources—many people use the same server and many servers are shared among the customer base. All of these elements make up a cloud solution—just the kind of thing that will be evaluated in this book.

This definition, while it works well for a public cloud solution like Facebook, Amazon Web Services, or LISHost, might need some tweaking to apply to a private cloud. Private clouds have all the always-on, convenient, no "hands-on" features that the public cloud does without the need to share those resources with the general public. The resources may well be shared among divisions of the library or even libraries in a consortium, but they are privately held resources that are not made available to the public. That's really the only difference between a public and private cloud.

Another term you may come across when looking at cloud services is the hybrid cloud. This is a cloud that is essentially either public or private but has an element of the other included. This could be a server that is owned by a library and mostly used within the library itself, but that also offers at least semipublic services such as hosted websites or community access to resources. It could also be a public cloud resource such as an Amazon Web Services account that is used both for public facing services and for private, internal services as well. All clouds—whether public, private, or hybrid—involve a vendor or provider or organization making networked resources available to others in an automated and automatic way.

All clouds are accessed through a client of some sort. Most clouds are browser-accessible. This means that anyone with an Internet connection and a browser (this includes most smartphones these days) can access the cloud services being offered. Some other cloud clients include something like thin client computers that offer relatively little computing power of their own, just a connection to a cloud service and a monitor. Other clients include mobile apps and terminal emulators (like the Putty program for Windows—http://www.putty.org) for access to lower-level types of cloud services such as the IaaS (Infrastructure as a Service) defined below.

Some of you may remember the thin client architecture of the early computing era. Thin clients were essentially monitors with some sort of input ability (a keyboard, usually) and access to a mainframe computer, and all computation and "heavy lifting" in terms of computing happened on the mainframe with the results being printed to the thin client's monitor. The current trend toward off-loading computing duties to the cloud is similar, but not quite the same. While browsers are, essentially, thin clients and the servers are, essentially, mainframes doing the computing, these days, thin clients aren't quite so thin. Browsers can do some computing on their own so that the server doesn't have to do all of the work all of the time and so that some work can be done when the connection to the server has been interrupted (such as Google Docs' offline mode). When the connection is restored, the browser syncs its information with the data on the server and work continues as before. Even modern smartphones have more computing power than a traditional thin client, so they can also do some work offline and sync up when back in service. Even though some of the terms may bring back memories for those of you who lived through the mainframe days of computing, the use of thin clients today is very different.

## ACRONYMS AND TYPES OF CLOUD SERVICES

There are many aaS-type services that are associated with the cloud. The aaS at the end of each of the next acronyms stands for "as a Service." This identifies the various services mentioned as cloud-based services.

**IaaS**—Infrastructure as a Service—provides infrastructure resources: file storage servers and load balancing servers and virtual machine servers as well as network appliances such as firewalls and software routers. These low-level services can be deployed and maintained through a browser with a connection to the cloud.

**PaaS**—Platform as a Service—provides platforms such as operating systems and web servers and databases or development tools. Where the IaaS replicates physical machines on the cloud, PaaS replicates the software that runs on servers and other high-end machines.

**SaaS**—Software as a Service—provides software such as office suites and graphical editing programs and just about any other kind of software you might need to use. SaaS generally refers to consumer-level software, where PaaS refers to IT-level software.

**STaaS**—Storage as a Service—provides file and data storage on a subscription basis. Unlike IaaS, where you are deploying a virtual hardware server to store your files, with STaaS, you "rent" only the space needed to store those files without regard to the background server or operating system that supports that storage.

**SECaaS**—Security as a Service—provides security tools such as authentication into a network, antivirus tools, and more on a subscription basis.

**DaaS**—Data as a Service—provides access to data stores without regard for the type of storage used—file or database—and usually includes the method of accessing that data in the package.

**TEaaS**—Test Environment as a Service—provides access to testing environments so that organizations can test out software and make changes to existing software without possibly damaging the production software that is in use.

**DaaS**—Desktop as a Service—provides a desktop environment for end users that is accessed through a browser or other thin client and is also known as desktop virtualization.

This book will examine examples of most of these kinds of cloud services and explain what it is that you, as the customer, should be looking for and how to determine which vendor in that particular service sector will work for your needs.

## CLOUD LIMITS

There are limitations to using the cloud—many of which I will detail in later sections of the book when discussing specific cloud services. For now, keep in mind that total reliance on the cloud means that when the Internet hiccups—and it will—you will be unable to access those cloud-based resources for which you are paying. Whether the hiccup is from a natural disaster–type of event or caused by a poor decision in the IT department of your vendor or even an outage by your own Internet service provider (ISP), any loss of network access will mean a loss of access to your data and files and information and software and so on.

This means that you should have some contractual agreement between you and your vendor about how much "downtime" is acceptable for both of you and what the vendor will do if the amount of downtime exceeds what you have determined is acceptable. Downtime—in this instance, at least—involves any loss of service to the cloud resources that is not the fault of your ISP or your local network. Downtime (or rather uptime, which is, as you may guess, the opposite of downtime) is usually defined by the "9's" standards. A very reliable service might guarantee five 9's of uptime (time when you do have access to your cloud resources), which is 99.999% up. This works out, for a service that runs 24/7, to about 5 1/4 minutes of downtime a year or 25 seconds a month. This is gold standard–level service, though not the absolute top tier of cloud services, and if you require this kind of guaranteed access to your resources, you should expect to pay a bit more. For three 9's (99.9%) service, you can expect about 8 3/4 hours of downtime a year or 44 minutes a month. More examples of uptime calculations can be found at the high availability page on Wikipedia (http://en.wikipedia.org/wiki/High_availability). Determining how much uptime or availability you need and how much downtime you can tolerate is one of the steps you will need to take before checking out cloud vendors. Once you decide on a number of hours you can live with, then you need to discuss with your vendor what they will do if those hours are exceeded. Some will give you credits to your account; some will offer other reparations—but do make sure you know what those are and check to make sure you are going to get something to make up for their issues if they prove to be less reliable than you might hope.

You also give up some control over software updates and patching with cloud-based software solutions. Sometimes you can completely configure your software to work for you, even if it's shared software that is in the SaaS (Software as a Service) part of the cloud—but rarely can you control the schedule of updates and patches and upgrades. If you need some specific feature of a software package and your provider isn't planning to upgrade for a while, you may just be out of luck. This is definitely something you need to consider for both risks in upgrading before all the bugs have been worked out of the software and risks in security and loss of functionality if the software isn't upgraded often enough. Your organization needs to determine what sort of schedule you will be comfortable with and, if the vendor does the upgrading, make sure you are both on the same page.

While cloud computing and cloud services can be excellent solutions for many of the problems your organization may be experiencing, it is not a panacea for every problem you might face. Keeping cloud solutions in mind is a good strategy, but realize that one solution will not fit all problems.

How do you decide if the cloud is the answer to your issues? Consider whether the issue is technological at all—some issues that your organization may have might be cultural. Much like buying a collaboration suite of software won't make your organization's culture automatically collaborative, putting resources on the cloud won't make your organization's culture automatically accepting of this sort of software. If your organization prizes individual work and locally held resources, a cloud solution that encourages collaboration won't work—no matter how technologically superior the solution might be.

Another issue may just be training. Many times switching to a cloud solution requires a drastic change in workflow or organizational duties—things that require more training and perhaps a complete overhaul of how the organization does work. Both of these issues—training and workflow—can make a cloud solution less than ideal when compared to using a more traditional solution. Even for software that doesn't require a change in workflow, more training may be needed to show folks how to get to the software and how to use it. Much of the cloud software that is out there now is pretty easy to use, but even easy-to-use software can require training to get people comfortable with using it.

The cloud has many benefits as well, enough to populate the entire next chapter, but before jumping headfirst into a cloud solution, I wanted to discuss some of the drawbacks. Along with determining what kinds of services you need to go to the cloud, spend some time determining what kind of risk you are willing to take in order to get some of the benefits that will be presented next and what sort of solution you really need—will a new technological service actually solve your problem? Once you've decided that the risks are worth it, you can start reaping the benefits of moving services and technologies in your library to the cloud.

*Chapter Two*

# Why Use the Cloud?

While every organization is different and will have different needs for their technology services, there are some universal "goods" that the cloud-based services presented in this book can address, many of which aren't really technological at all. Cloud services provide an easy way to maintain software in a very structured way and to collaborate with people both inside and outside of your organization, and they can be a big help in keeping costs from both hardware and software issues from skyrocketing. As your organization begins using the cloud for more and more services, you might find other benefits as well—many more than are mentioned in this chapter.

## CLOUD BENEFITS

Keeping in mind the downfalls of using the cloud, I will continue by listing some of the benefits that working in the cloud and using cloud services can provide to an organization.

### Upgrades and Patches

One of the limitations that I noted in the last chapter can also be a benefit, depending on how you look at it. In chapter 1, I pointed out that most cloud providers do upgrades and patching of the software that you are using without any intervention required from you. If you don't have an IT staff yourself—or your IT staff is seriously overworked—this could be a good thing. It is one less thing that your organization's staff will have to consider. As long as you are assured that patches and upgrades are being done in order to keep your software system safe, you can pretty much ignore that part of the software ownership responsibility and concentrate on learning to use the software as efficiently and easily as possible.

Other, related benefits include possibly getting improvements and new features faster than you could manage yourself and getting upgrades done by people who know what they are doing and have done this sort of thing before. Often, when upgrading software, the individual IT person or department will wait to see what kinds of problems others have before they do the upgrade themselves. Alternatively, if they don't wait, they may run into issues and problems with which they have no experience. A vendor that manages many different organizations' software packages would avoid both of these issues, for the most part. They would have much more experience in the software and the upgrade path because they do it for so many different clients.

## Collaboration

Another benefit that I mentioned earlier is the ability to easily collaborate with others using the decentralized nature of cloud services. Instead of creating a document using a local word-processing program and having that document live on one computer with one person having access to it, you can create documents using a cloud service like Google Drive or Zoho Office and make them accessible to anyone with the correct permissions (including not requiring permissions at all—making it fully accessible to the world). This makes collaborating among different people—especially different people at different organizations who might be using different word-processing software—very easy. While it won't make your organization automatically a collaborative organization, it will make it easier to consider sharing information and ideas with others!

Another form of collaboration that is especially popular in libraries is the forming of consortia. Libraries in Missouri have banded together in order to use the cloud-based Overdrive software, getting a break on the price compared to if they had chosen to go it alone. Libraries in Kansas have collaborated on the 3M cloud library software—they decided to use a different software service, but for many of the same reasons. Other libraries collaborate on shared catalogs and a variety of other library-specific software for a variety of reasons. Both the output of the software (documents in the case of Google Drive) and the software itself (the 3M library software in the case of the Kansas libraries) can be a tool for collaboration and a pooling of resources to give all libraries—regardless of their size—a shot at the same kinds of services that big libraries can afford to manage on their own.

One of the side benefits of the same features that allow for easy collaboration is the improvement of productivity. If the documents are all in a central place, updated and version controlled—as each of the cloud office software services mentioned in chapter 6 are—there is no time lost to hunting around in e-mail attachments, looking for the latest version of a document, or in working on an old version by accident. Your staff has access to the very latest version of any document in a centralized storage area. No one person can monopolize the information or act as a bottleneck by getting the document and then neglecting to add his or her part, holding up the process for everyone involved.

## Budgets

Another benefit is budgetary. Often (though not always) renting software to use via the cloud can be cheaper than buying it outright and then dealing with the licensing costs, the per-client usage costs, the staff management time costs, and whatever other costs may come from the licensing of software. Usually there is an economy of scale that makes cloud-based software less expensive than the desktop-based versions. While you may have to give up some bits of functionality, often you may discover that the functionality being lost is something that is used only rarely and by just a few people. Those people can have full desktop versions of the software while everyone else uses the cloud version, if that proves to be the case.

There are less tangible benefits to the bottom-line budget of an organization as well. Since staff aren't required to patch or upgrade the software, you can save on personnel costs. Since collaboration encourages productivity, you get more out of your staff than in a more traditional workflow. Since collaboration itself is encouraged, you get the benefits of multiple points of view and multiple brains working on a problem for your organization. That sort of thinking can be priceless.

Related to budgets, sort of, is the issue of regulatory compliance. Many governmental agencies—some of which are libraries—have requirements to store or make documentation available to the public as requested. Sunshine laws and requirements for storing e-mail and other "official" documents mean that some libraries could have a pretty big pile of data they need to maintain. Cloud storage and document management tools could be of help in that situation by giving the library a way to store that information that is both cost-effective and easily accessible.

## Application Programming Interfaces

Each cloud service that you use will provide some way to integrate itself with the other cloud services via an API (application programming interface). APIs give you a hook into a software service. Examples would be the Google Maps API, which lets website developers add mapping functionality to their sites by calling functions of Google Maps via an API that Google has made available. Some services do a better job of this than others, but most provide some sort of way into the service so that you (or someone who has some programming experience) can weave together your various cloud-based services and applications so that they work together more smoothly. Traditional installed software rarely offered this sort of integration between installed programs—occasionally Adobe will release a plug-in that works with Microsoft Office or something like that, but it's entirely dependent on what the software creators decide to do and how they decide to work together. Cloud services, on the other hand, give much more control to the customer by making certain functions completely available via a programmatical interface—an API. APIs and how to work with them are well beyond the scope of this book, but there have been books written about how to use them in libraries that you can consult (see *Library Mashups*, edited by Nicole Engard and published by Information Today in 2009) for more information on "mashing together" the various services you use so that they can work together in a somewhat seamless manner.

Every organization will give each benefit mentioned in this chapter a different weight based on what is most important to them—some will be swayed toward using the cloud strictly because of the budgetary benefits; others may prefer the ease of maintenance or the collaborative benefits that cloud-based software can provide. Other organizations might have completely different benefits—regulatory requirements that are more easily met with cloud-based software, for example.

Overall, using the cloud is a way to off-load some IT headaches and potentially save some money, so many of you are going to want to do it. This book will go through several different categories of cloud services and discuss the best way to evaluate and decide on a particular cloud vendor or service for your organization. Each subsequent chapter will focus on a particular sector of the cloud computing services that are available today and will go through the process of how to evaluate them—helping you to decide what features are most important to your organization and what risks are too big to take.

*Chapter Three*

# ILS in the Cloud

One of the most important pieces of technology in any library is the ILS—the integrated library system. This is the system that manages the library's stock of books, movies, and other materials as well as the system that keeps track of patrons and what they have checked out. Because this is a very important part of any library, it can be nerve-racking to outsource even parts of it. Any connectivity issue between your library and the vendor can mean that your library is unable to access some or all of your ILS functions—including circulation and the online catalog. Most ILSs, however, offer some "offline" capabilities that give libraries some peace of mind when it comes to Internet outages and other issues. This maturation of the services offered by cloud ILS vendors has led some libraries to begin using cloud-based ILS products successfully right now. Jason Griffey of the University of Tennessee in Chattanooga led a migration of his library's ILS to one of the first real "cloud" solutions—WorldCat Web Management by OCLC.

Other library services that can be off-loaded to the cloud include hosted link resolvers (connections between citations and the articles or other resources being cited) and hosted proxy servers (authentication gateways for off-site users). For each of these catalog- and database-related services, alternatives to the traditional installed services exist. We'll look at those alternatives and what to keep an eye out for when deciding if to use them and what to use for your organization.

## INTEGRATED LIBRARY SYSTEM IN THE CLOUD

The things to consider when deciding whether to move your ILS from a locally hosted product—which most libraries use today—to a product that lives in the cloud include bandwidth requirements, privacy and security issues, and what particular features you must have in a hosted ILS. You need to be sure that your Internet connection is both reliable enough and big enough to handle the extra data that will be going between your library and the cloud for every single transaction that occurs in your building. Privacy and security are entwined; good security practices by both you and your chosen vendor will help protect your patrons' privacy. Chapter 12 deals entirely with staying secure in the cloud—be sure to read that chapter to make sure you are doing all the right things security-wise. The features you will need, including modules like acquisitions or serials or extras like support levels, need to be determined before you begin looking for a cloud ILS vendor. Make sure you know what you absolutely need to function before you start looking at features of these ILS software packages—in this case, at least, surprises are not a good thing.

Once those major issues are sorted out, then you can begin to look at what options are out there and if any of them will work for you. Find out if anyone near you is using the product and see what they think of it. Keep an eye on Jason Griffey's blog, Pattern Recognition (http://jasongriffey.net/wp/). In it he discusses the results of a bunch of his technical projects, including updates on how the University of Tennessee is doing with their hosted ILS. Don't just rely on his reports, though—he has a technical team he leads; if you don't have anyone helping you, you may find some of his challenges would be outright obstacles for you. Find out if other libraries your size are using a hosted ILS and pick their brains. Find out what kind of technical team they have in place, if any, and what sort of problems they've encountered while they have been using the cloud ILS. This may be somewhat difficult at first—there aren't a lot of libraries out there that are using purely cloud-based ILSs yet, but by the time this book is published, there should be more and more coming online all the time.

## Players in the Cloud ILS Arena

The big player right now—the first on the scene, really—is OCLC World-Share Management Services. This is a full-featured ILS that is hosted in the cloud by OCLC. The latest information on the service can be found at http://www.oclc.org/webscale/default.htm. As of late 2012, the service offered all of the modules that traditional ILSs offer—cataloging, acquisitions, license management, and circulation, among others—and included collaborative functions built into the system. Libraries that use WorldShare Management Services can share cataloging and other tasks with other WorldShare libraries, cutting the amount of work to be done by any one library and allowing libraries to catalog, acquire, and circulate materials as collaboratively as they like.

The other major players on the scene are less specifically cloud-based ILSs as they are accidental ones. The Evergreen ILS was built for consortia use, so it was meant to be centrally served and accessed by multiple libraries, though it was never really built as a cloud-based application. The latest information about Evergreen can be found at http://www.open-ils.org/. Evergreen is an open-source ILS, meaning the software itself is free for anyone to use. A group in Missouri, the MOBIUS consortium (http://mobiusconsortium.org), is using Evergreen for their union catalog, as are many other consortia around the world. Most libraries, unless they have significant programming expertise in-house, prefer to purchase a support contract from one of the many companies that have sprung up in this space. Some companies offer everything from hosting to day-to-day management; others offer smaller packages that include some level of service that is agreeable to both the vendor and the library. All of those support packages cost, but they are generally less expensive than a traditional ILS, so they are becoming popular. Koha, another open-source ILS, was intended for single-library use but is successfully used in consortia around the country, such as in the NEKLS (North East Kansas Library System at http://catalog.nexpresslibrary.org), which had, as of the end of 2012, approximately forty libraries using a centrally located and managed server. Both open-source ILSs require either a lot of technical skills on your organization's end or a support contract that does cost—but is usually less than a traditional in-house ILS by a large margin.

One traditional ILS vendor who now has a cloud-hosted offering for libraries is SirsiDynix. Their Symphony ILS can be either installed traditionally in-house or can be hosted by SirsiDynix as a cloud-based ILS. It has comparable features to the previous cloud-based ILS options and is something to look at if your library was previously a SirsiDynix customer or if you want the support and structure of a traditional ILS vendor without the headaches and issues of hosting the ILS in your own organization.

One other player that is just coming onto the scene as this book is being written is Librarika (http://librarika.com/). It is a fully online, fully cloud-based ILS that is geared toward smaller libraries (up to two thousand records is free; beyond that number does have some costs) and is still building out some features at this time (early summer of 2013). They offer, besides the traditional back-end staff modules, front-end OPAC features, and the benefits of cloud-based hosting, space for storage of e-books that the library owns. For libraries that have been fighting to own their e-content, this could be a big selling point in this start-up's favor. As with many of the cloud-based options you have, a free trial is easy to work out—just choose a smallish collection in your library, one that is less than two thousand records, and use Librarika to manage that collection for a bit. Use the OPAC to find items in the collection, use the back-end modules to manage the inventory aspects and the acquisition of new materials for the collection, and get a sense of whether this particular ILS will work for you. As with many cloud-based services, importing and exporting your data to and from the ILS is reasonably simple and can make testing out this kind of service much easier and less traumatic than changing to a full-blown ILS that might or might not work well with your patrons, staff, and workflow.

Other ILSs—both closed and open source—will be on the market and in the cloud soon. Remember that you can always look around to find someone else who uses the product and who can tell you how it works for their library. Remember, too, though, that you have to take into account their organization's size, technical competency, and budgetary flexibility. If those things aren't the same as your situation, you might find yourself with problems you didn't anticipate. Other than that, make sure that the solution you choose has all the features you need as well as all of the support you will require. Asking for a demonstration that you can actually put your hands on should not be too difficult. Vendors should be able to give you access to a demo account and let you play with it without too much trouble. If you can get this, take advantage of it—kick the tires and try your very best to make it fail. Your patrons will assuredly do the same once you have it installed and live in your library. Also check to see what vendor your ILS is using to host in the cloud. There are some that use commercial services such as Amazon's EC2 Virtual Servers and others that use dedicated servers at hosting companies such as Rackspace. The differences in reliability can be pretty wide, so finding out who will be the final host of your system and checking out their reliability in the past may be something you will want to do before signing a contract with a vendor. This advice holds true for other add-ons in the ILS space, too, such as hosted link resolvers and hosted proxy servers.

## HOSTED LINK RESOLVERS

Connections between the catalog and the databases that a library owns can be managed through link resolvers. A link resolver is a bit of software that takes citations from one page on the web (a database, a catalog page, etc.) and connects that citation to the full text of the article in a database. Many libraries use link resolvers to make their patrons' lives a bit easier: patrons can tell when an article is available in a library-owned database in full text and go straight there without having to search that database first. This software can be locally installed and managed, or it can be hosted externally and function as a cloud application.

Two of the better known hosted link resolvers are Ex Libris's SFX (http://www.exlibrisgroup.com/category/SFXOverview) and 360 Link by Serials Solutions (http://www.serialssolutions.com/en/services/360-link). They are

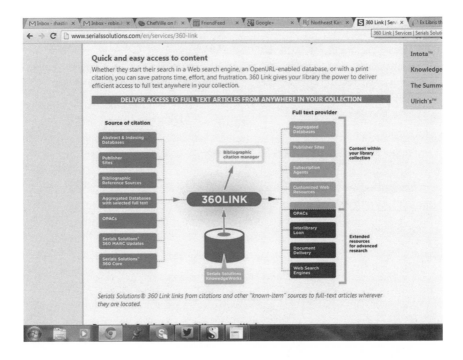

**Figure 3.1.   Screenshot of the home page of 360 Link by Serials Solutions showing just how link resolvers work.**

both available as hosted solutions that can be customized to fit a particular library's needs. Choosing the hosted version of a link resolver—whichever one you choose—gives you the same sort of benefits you get from any hosted software: less IT maintenance required, less money spent, and less strain on the library's internal resources in both staff and the actual machines required to run the service. You also get the same sort of issues with hosted software, though: less ability to completely customize, less control over the service itself, and just as much of a learning curve to get it configured and working.

## HOSTED PROXY SERVERS

Proxy servers give people located outside the library building—for public libraries—or off campus—for academic libraries—access to the library's resources and databases. Many database vendors require that only people within a certain location can access a library's databases. Proxy servers let people from outside of that location use their library credentials (library card and PIN or password) to fool those databases into thinking they are being accessed from the approved location. EZproxy is one of the most popular proxy

**Easily extendable**

In addition to using all the functionality that SFX provides, you can create your own functionality! SFX is an open system, and many customers create code extensions and share them with the whole community via the EL Commons collaborative Web site. SFX i highly interoperable through open interfaces, allowing seamless integration with other systems in the library.

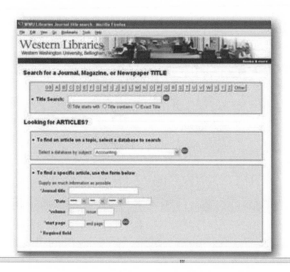

**Figure 3.2.   Screenshot of the home page of the Ex Libris SFX Link Resolver showing options for Ex Libris's link resolver.**

servers in use today, and there are a couple of vendors that offer hosted—or cloud-based—EZproxy services. They will set up, configure, and host an EZproxy proxy server for you so that your patrons can use your resources remotely without much hassle for either your patrons or your staff.

Even though the most popular proxy server in use in libraries today is the EZproxy server, you still have choices if you decide to host your EZproxy server in the cloud—there are several vendors who specialize in hosting EZproxy for organizations. Two of them are Datacom (http://www. datacominc.com/ezproxy.html) and OCLC (http://www.oclc.org/ezproxy/ hosted/default.htm). Whichever you go with, the benefits of hosting your EZproxy implementation would be the same—it's just a matter of which vendor suits your needs and budget the best.

While the purchasing, installing, and maintaining of the ILS, link resolver, and proxy server is still the mainstream choice today, it is becoming more and more likely that, in the future, you will be renting access to this software instead. The companies and services offered in this book are just the tip of the iceberg when it comes to the options that libraries have in the hosted/cloud-based library software arena. As more libraries come to the end of life on their hardware, they will face this decision. If your library is in that position, remember to evaluate your needs carefully, talk to libraries of a similar size and with similar resources to determine what solution will fit you best, and do your homework by researching the features and support offered by each of the vendors you consider.

*Chapter Four*

# Web Hosting in the Cloud

Most organizations outsource their web hosting. Contracting with an outside vendor as a web host is actually hosting in the cloud most of the time. Your site is being hosted in one of the many server farms located somewhere in the United States (usually), but you don't know where. You don't get to go visit your server nor do you really care where it is. That is the way websites have traditionally been hosted, so cloud-based web hosting won't be anything new to most of you. Because of this, I'll spend a bit more time in this chapter talking about the pros and cons of "insourcing" your website—hosting it in your physical building as opposed to hosting your site in the cloud. Of course, the library's website isn't the only thing you might want to serve to your patrons (or not serve, as the case may be)—web content filtering is a requirement for many libraries these days and many vendors offer hosted, off-site filtering services. Content is another aspect of the site that can be cloud-hosted, even if the rest of your site is kept in-house. In this chapter, I'll talk about video hosting, specifically, but other bits of content, such as images in Flickr or Facebook, can be displayed on your website while being hosted in the cloud.

One of the major benefits of being able to use the cloud with web hosting is the ability to pull data and content from multiple places and have it all live together on one page. To your patrons, it appears that everything is living happily together while your website structure may be hosted on an Amazon virtual server, your pictures on Flickr, and at least some of your content coming from your cloud-based ILS. Of course, you could just put everything on a single server and serve it from a single place, but then you get into duplicated content and effort—why re-create data about your materials that you own if you can just pull that data directly from the catalog? Why host a picture or video locally, with all of the storage and bandwidth issues that incurs, when Flickr or Kaltura can host it and you can let them deal with those issues? Why keep your website in your building and face the headaches of a publicly facing server and all the security issues that go along with it when you can have Amazon or Rackspace or LISHost deal with all of that? Of course, cloud hosting is rarely free, but when compared with the costs of purchasing, licensing, and maintaining a server in your building, it's most often cheaper than doing it yourself. Web hosts get economies of scale that individual hosts just can't match.

## WEB-HOSTING OPTIONS

The basics of hosting—what server platform you will use—are pretty straightforward. If you plan to use (or have in-house talent in) a particular programming or web scripting language like .Net or ASP (Active Server Pages), you may want to find a web host that runs the Windows server and the IIS (Internet Information Services) software. This is probably going to be a bit more expensive than a Linux server running Apache, but if you already have someone who will be able to take advantage of the aforementioned Windows Server technologies—.Net and ASP—then it could very well save you money in the long run. Server technology is nearly always cheaper than programming skill. On the other hand, if you have someone who has experience with PHP—a web scripting language that runs Drupal, Wordpress, and many other open-source and free server software packages—or experience with one of those software packages like Wordpress, you will be best served by getting a Linux-based server running the Apache web server software. If you will be outsourcing the design, maintenance, or content creation for your site, go with Linux and Apache. The software is free, there are a number of popular and well-known server software packages that are also free, and the price per hour of people with skill sets that will be able to help you out is lower (in general) than a comparable Microsoft Windows–based skill set.

Once you have done your evaluation and you know what kind of server you wish to get, you can determine if the server should be in the cloud or in-house. The big benefits to having a server in-house are control and the possibility of a quick response. With the server physically sitting in the building, you have ultimate control over that server and how it works. That can be good or it can be scary, depending on your comfort level with server-side technology. You can also get to the server and respond to outages quickly, perhaps more quickly than a cloud server situation even. The downsides to these are the fact that if something goes wrong, you are responsible for fixing it when it happens—even if that is in the middle of the night or while you are on vacation. Cloud hosting takes the issues of fixing hardware failures or power outage instances away and spreads those duties among several people who won't all be on vacation at the same time, generally.

You also have to consider the traffic that hosting a website can put on your network. If you have a reasonably popular site, the amount of bandwidth needed to keep that site responding quickly and keep your other computers from bogging down can be expensive. Off-loading those issues to a cloud provider can prove to be a cheaper option, even with the monthly or yearly rental fees for that cloud server, since web-hosting companies can buy bandwidth and capacity at generally lower rates due to the volume of bandwidth and capacity they are purchasing. Even if you plan for enough bandwidth for everyday use, if something happens to make your library's website very popular—a news story pointing to the site or some national event happening at your library—you may not be able to quickly ramp up to handle the extra traffic. Most cloud-based web hosts can—it will cost you extra, but they can do it quickly and seamlessly.

Once you've decided to go with a cloud-hosted website and finished the evaluation of either your current website (what content you have and what format it is in) or your needs for a website if you don't already have one, the next big decision is who will host the site. The web-hosting field is large and crowded. There are a lot of commercial hosts that can and will host a site for a very reasonable charge.

Some of the bigger web hosts are Dreamhost (http://www.dreamhost.com/r.cgi?1366360/servers/compare-our-products/), Hostgator (http://www.hostgator.com/shared), and Bluehost (http://www.bluehost.com/tell_me_more.html). They provide more support and are generally geared toward people who are not professional web developers, so they will have niceties like CPanel or Plesk. CPanel and Plesk are both web server graphical user interfaces (GUIs)—they provide a point-and-click way to manage a server and are very handy for managing web servers. Most servers, without some sort of GUI installed, are configured through the editing of text files via the command line. Using the command line is a very efficient way to manage a server, if you have hard-core command-line Linux skills. If not, using a GUI for your web server is a great way to get access to all of those configuration files with point-and-click ease.

If you want more value and less hand-holding in regard to server configuration, you can "rent" a cloud server from Rackspace (http://www.rackspace.com/) or Amazon (http://aws.amazon.com). Both offer full-fledged servers with complete control of the environment for very reasonable prices. They generally provide a bare-bones machine that you have to then configure via that command line mentioned above. Again, this is great if you have the in-house skills for that, but difficult to manage if you don't. Another benefit that going with a cloud server such as Amazon or Rackspace will provide is pay-as-you-go pricing schemes. You pay for the amount of server resources you use and no more. With the more traditional web hosts, you are locked into a set price each month or year for a set amount of server space and bandwidth. With a pure cloud provider like Amazon, you pay for the amount of system resources you use. For smaller sites this can be a substantial savings. For larger sites, this can provide some flexibility without huge overage costs, should an article on your site or an event involving your library make your site very popular.

Finally, if you want a web host that is already hosting a bunch of library websites and has a bunch of experience with libraries and their needs, you could go with LISHost (http://www.lishost.org) for a web server at a reasonable price and plenty of hand-holding and support to go with it. Blake Carver, the owner of LISHost, is also very much interested in web and cloud security—see the interview with him in chapter 12, the cloud security chapter—and as such will help to keep your sites secure, something that general web hosts tend to leave to your organization to manage.

## WHEN YOU DON'T HAVE TIME TO CREATE CONTENT

One thing that outsourcing or cloud-sourcing a website cannot do is create content for your site. No matter how much you might wish, the content is going to have to come from your organization and only from your organization. While you can gather print materials and hand them off to a copywriter to massage into web-appropriate content and you can hire a photographer to go around taking pictures of your events, staff, and facilities, the origination of the content must come from you. No one else knows what you want on your site or what your patrons want from your site (although a good web designer will do some user testing to try to determine what patrons might want on your site, they have to have some basic information from you to start). You can, however, take very minimal content—your contact information, hours of operation, and a link to your catalog—and place a "one-pager" up as your home on the web. For some smaller libraries, that may be just exactly what you need.

One-pagers from Influx, a library-focused user experience and web design company, can be a solution for small libraries with little content that needs to be online, but who want to have a home on the web anyway. The one-pager web templates that Influx designs (information about them can be found at http://influx.us/onepager/) provide a simple and very cost-effective way to put your content online. The template that Influx provides is free— you can download it without cost. For a bit of money, they will help you implement it, but if you have basic HTML skills and a web host on standby, you can easily add your information and make it your home page on the web for zero cost. This still requires you to provide your content, but your content can be as simple as a picture, your address and hours of operation, and a couple of relevant links. No more content is required for this kind of basic website to be useful for your organization.

## WEB CONTENT FILTERING

Web content filtering is controversial. Many librarians feel that it is contrary to what they are supposed to do as librarians—provide a gateway to content, rather than act as a content guard—but many librarians are also in the position of either filtering their public computers or not being able to afford to provide any Internet access at all. If your organization is in that position, instead of performing the evaluation of your environment that I recommend for just about every other cloud-based service mentioned here, you will want to create policies for filtering that are going to both follow the law and provide as much information to patrons as possible. Once you have policies in place, getting a cloud-based web filtering service will be the easy part.

In Missouri, the MORENet organization—provider of Internet services to Missouri government, schools, and libraries—offers a cloud-hosted Netsweeper implementation. They host the Netsweeper filter, and because they provide the Internet service, they can easily insert the filter between the wider Internet and each customer who needs to use it. For the cost of the service—which is based on the number of computers being filtered—customers get access to fine-tune the filters via a web-based control panel, but avoid having to purchase, configure, and maintain a piece of hardware or software that would do the same thing within their own network. MORENet provides the hardware, initial configuration, and ongoing maintenance of the service; customers of the service just have to pay the yearly bill and fine-tune the filter to fit their policies—something that is a matter of clicking the appropriate checkboxes in a web form, really. More information on the cloud-hosted features and services from MORENet can be found at http://www.more.net/content/internet-content-filtering-morenet-hosted. Other states may have similar programs—check with your local libraries to see if they know of anything or check in with your local consortium to see if they are providing any kind of filtering service for their libraries.

A statewide initiative in Maine brings most school districts and libraries into a cloud-hosted filtering service called OpenDNS. The story announcing that initiative ran at the Center for Digital Education's website, found at http://www.centerdigitaled.com/infrastructure/Maine-Moves-to-Cloud-Based-Internet-Filtering-for-Public-Schools-Libraries.html. OpenDNS is a service that provides security in several different ways—one of which is cloud-based Internet content filtering. Content filtering can help keep malware (software that does bad things to your computer and/or your computer's network) and other undesirable software out of libraries by cutting off access to sites known to host it. That is one benefit that many libraries saw after implementing content filtering at their locations. More information on the OpenDNS services can be found at http://www.umbrella.com/umbrella-security-is-for-everyone/#education.

Untangle (http://wiki.untangle.com/index.php/Web_Filter), a software platform that allows users to create network-based applications (such as content filters), is another option for do-it-yourself cloud-hosted web filtering. Using a private or hybrid cloud, you could set up Untangle to work for several libraries in a consortium or for a large library with many branches spread throughout a geographical area. For the consortium, the folks managing the network would be the cloud vendors while the member libraries would be "customers" using the service. For the large library, the IT department would be both vendor and customer—as is common with a private cloud. Either way, the Untangle software is freely available (open source) and would be a reasonable choice for a library or library group with in-house server-side management talent.

## VIDEO HOSTING

While there are many options for content hosting out there—Flickr or Picasa for images, Scribd for documents, and Delicious for links and bundled content—one of the more useful kinds of content hosting is video hosting. Images, documents, and link collections are fairly small, in terms of mega- or gigabytes served to the patron upon request for those things. Video, on the other hand, is frequently one of the larger bits of content that a library can provide. Multiple requests for that content, served from the library's own network, can slow down a network quickly—even bringing it to a screeching halt if the video gets popular enough. There are several options for video hosting—each one with pros and cons.

YouTube and Vimeo are generally free and pretty easy to use—though both of them will show commercials that you may or may not have any control over. A paid solution like Kaltura, on the other hand, is also pretty easy to use and will forgo the commercials in exchange for payment for their services. Baruch College, in New York City, is one customer of Kaltura. As seen in the screenshot below, they have quite a bit of video that they contract with Kaltura to host for them so that Kaltura gets the bandwidth hit each time someone requests a new video. You can see the whole set of Baruch College videos at https://baruch.mediaspace.kaltura.com/.

Web hosting in the cloud can be complicated. Pulling content from Flickr or Kaltura into a website that is hosted by Amazon and into a network that filters the content of the Internet using Untangle means that you have many

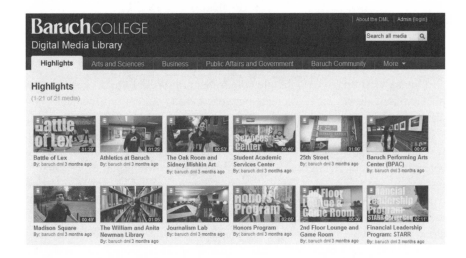

**Figure 4.1. Videos created by Baruch College and hosted on Kaltura's video-hosting servers.**

different ways that everything can go wrong. With the cloud-hosted website and content model, there are multiple points of failure in a single website. Adding social media widgets and other content that lives outside of the actual website adds more points of failure. Despite these drawbacks, however, the cost and efficiency of the cloud-hosted website model are making it more and more popular with all kinds of organizations. The reduced costs and increased content possibilities make the model attractive, especially for organizations that have limited resources. However you decide to make your website available to the public, chances are some part of it will come from the cloud and you will find yourself and your organization managing cloud-based resources in some way. (See chapter 10 for more information on using social media in the cloud and on your website.)

*Chapter Five*

# Cloud Backups

Backups are a modern fact of life for every organization that has any kind of computing technology (and that is all of them these days). Every organization needs to back up their data in case of technological or user errors. Traditional backups have been done using an internal or external tape drive that takes magnetic tapes (minicassettes) and writes the compressed data from the server onto the tape. These tapes are neither cheap nor fast and require a human being to move them around. From changing tapes on a daily basis to moving tapes out of the initial location in case of major damage to the library's building (think earthquake or tornado), they are pretty labor-intensive—at least in comparison to a backup solution that takes advantage of always-on Internet access and low-bandwidth times during the night to run a backup copy of the data and send it, via the Internet, to the cloud.

## BACKUP OPTIONS

For smaller organizations that only have computer workstations, with no in-house servers to back up, something like Dropbox (http://www.dropbox.com) or Box.net (http://www.box.net) would work to back up important files on each computer. Installation of the client for both backup providers is point-and-click easy, and once the Dropbox or Box.net folder is in place, remembering to store documents that you want backed up in that folder is the extent of the brainpower required to make sure your data is both safe in a physically removed location (the backup providers' servers in the cloud) and easily recoverable (both services allow you to log into the website from any computer and redownload your data at any time). Both services mentioned here have free options that run from 2GB of data to 5GB of data and both offer more storage for a relatively small fee. These sorts of services are ideal for very small libraries that simply have a few staff members who need to be able to back up their documents and important files easily.

For larger libraries that have in-house servers and a more complicated technological setup, the general idea is the same, but their backup solution may be costlier and more complex than the smaller library's. Most libraries that have servers in their buildings use those servers for file sharing and domain controlling purposes—as well as for many other purposes from website hosting to ILS management to running displays throughout the library. All of these server functions are important to libraries, and all must be protected in the event of a tornado or system administrator with fumbling fingers. The Missouri River Regional Library—a midsized public library with several servers that perform domain controller, file sharing, website serving, and display management services—used to use traditional tape backups that would have to be changed on a daily basis and on a twice-weekly basis would be sent out to their branch library twenty miles away for physical security purposes. Today, they do none of that. They have switched to cloud backups for all of the computers in the library and, for just a bit more money than buying tapes, have completely eliminated the need for anyone to fuss with backups at all.

When it comes time to buy a new set of magnetic tapes to use for your backups and/or it becomes necessary to replace one of your servers, that is an excellent time to check out the possibility of using the cloud to back up your data and avoid the purchase of more tapes and/or a tape drive for a new server. There are a number of vendors out there willing and able to provide libraries with backup solutions—but those solutions are sometimes difficult to compare and require that you have a pretty good idea of everything you are backing up so that your organization can accurately gauge the storage you will need.

AUDIT YOURSELF!

Evaluation of all of your current backups is a good first step—go through each server or look at each individual computer that needs to be backed up, whichever your environment warrants, to determine the size of the monthly backups. The monthly backups usually, if following best practices for backups, consist of a full backup every Sunday evening, with incremental backups of just the changed data the other six nights of the week. All backups should be stored for a month, then overwritten on the tape or on the cloud storage space to which you are backing up your data. Using Windows Server's built-in backup utility, you can see the backups and how much space they were using on the disk. For Linux servers, a simple check of the backup file via command line will give you the size of your backup files. Combine all the backups done for all the servers or for all the computers—whichever you have—to get a starting point for comparing various backup services. Beyond just storage, though, if you want to send that data off-site to the cloud vendor's server, you have to make sure the bandwidth necessary to do so will be available overnight. Generally, the best practice is to start the transfer of data each night shortly after closing time to give yourself plenty of time to send all your data before opening again the next morning. If your library is open 24/7, though, you may have to identify exactly when your slowest times are to determine when you send those backups to avoid slowing down the Internet for your users.

Most backup vendors have two pricing points. They charge for total storage (the numbers you got from the backup utility in Windows or from adding together the amount of file space required for backup files in Linux) and the transfer of data between the server and the vendor. That number you may need to give an educated guess about to begin with, though many of the services do offer a "free trial" that will run the backups for a month or so and give you all the data you need to make your decision. The vendors' prices are generally close, but the features and services they offer vary pretty widely.

Most backup providers will give you a free client to install in your server in order to manage the backups. Some will offer a fee-based installation and tuning service that will help you set up your backups in a way that is less costly in both storage and data transfer. Others offer multiple layers of redundancy and security for your data. Some will give you multiple ways to recover data (online, through a mailed CD or DVD or hard drive of data, locally, etc.); others only offer a couple of those.

When I did this for my library, I asked around to see what other folks were using for their vendors and selected a few to try out. The vendors I fully evaluated were:

- MozyPro (http://mozy.com/pro);
- CrashPlan PRO (http://www.crashplanpro.com); and
- MORENet (http://www.more.net—this one is available only to MORENet customers in Missouri).

Others include JungleDisk (https://www.jungledisk.com/), which is based on Amazon's servers, and Carbonite (http://www.carbonite.com). I ended up with the three above because I needed to be able to make a decision—not necessarily because those three were better than Carbonite or JungleDisk.

The major features I was looking for in a cloud backup system were ease of installation, data compression at the client (to cut down on the amount of data being sent between my library and the storage server), and price. Most of what we were backing up consisted of documents and website files—nothing that required extraordinary levels of security—but if you are backing up patron information, you will want to add security assurances to that list of features for your organization. After installing clients, testing each service, and checking the pricing, I decided on CrashPlan PRO for our backup needs.

## MY LIBRARY'S DECISION

CrashPlan PRO offers clients for Windows, Mac, and Linux, so it would work on any computer or server we chose to use and it offered an "unlimited" plan that charged per server, rather than per data. This reassured me because the price would be steady all the time; even if our PR department decided to drop a bunch of heavy graphics into the file share server, the amount we pay each month would be static. In the beginning, the library paid for three servers—two file/domain controller servers that both backed up to an external hard drive and counted as one for CrashPlan PRO's purposes, our web server, and a file share server we have in a separate administration building. With a new virtualization setup, though, we now have combined the two domain controllers and file share server with the web server and they are all one physical server, cutting our costs down to two backed-up servers and costing us about $15 per month. Considering that the library was paying $60 every six months for tapes and buying tape drives for each server provisioned, our backup costs didn't go up very much at all—and if you add in the time not spent moving tapes around, they may have actually gone down.

After installing the client in the various servers and pointing to the folders that I wanted backed up, I haven't had to deal with backups at all—except to restore a file or two that got accidentally deleted by staff. Recovery—another feature that differentiates various cloud backup vendors—should be easily accomplished. With CrashPlan PRO, because the servers first back up to a local data storage site (this can be a USB hard drive, a spot on the server itself, or a full-fledged storage device that does nothing but collect backup files on your network), recovery for unintentionally deleted files is easy—just access the local backup through the provided client and find the file that was deleted from the actual server and click "restore." It is immediately placed back in the location from which it was deleted and you are now the library's hero.

More extensive backups are available, though, if there is a catastrophic event at your library. CrashPlan PRO offers both network and hard copy backups. This means that you can recover your data over the network or, if you are backing up large quantities of data and a network backup would take both too long and too much of your bandwidth, they will send you a hard copy of your data on disk, if necessary.

## A RECAP OF THE PROCESS

The process I went through was pretty much standard:

- Determine what vendors are being used by your peers.
- Determine what features you need for your library.
- Determine what features the various vendors offer.
- Determine price points for the features you need.
- Test each final vendor for ease of use, client installation flexibility, and recovery options.
- Choose the winning vendor and set up their client; then forget about it altogether (except for the daily e-mails that inform you of what the back-ups did the night before).

The choices I made were the ones that were best for the library at which I worked at the time. Your library will be different and your choices will be as well. As long as you do a thorough evaluation of your library's needs, find a vendor that meets those needs at a price you can afford, and follow the directions to install and initialize your new cloud backups, you will be able to "set it and forget it" when it comes to even the very important IT task of managing backups for your library.

*Chapter Six*

# Software as a Service (SaaS)

SaaS—aka Software as a Service—is a rapidly growing part of the cloud landscape and is something—like hosted website servers—that your organization probably already uses. If you use Gmail or Outlook Mail (formerly known as Hotmail) or Yahoo!, and you check that mail via their website, you use a cloud-based e-mail client. Even if you check that e-mail through a client installed on your computer—Outlook or Thunderbird or some other mail client—you are still using cloud-based mail services. If you ever write up a document using Google Drive or Zoho Office or Office 360, you are using a cloud-based alternative to traditionally client-based office productivity software. Many other examples exist—from online graphic editors like Picasa in Google+ to online games like Yahoo! Games' Chess. Many of the software packages that used to exclusively be available to those who had the ability to purchase them, the ability to download them onto a personal computer, and the knowledge required to run them are now freely (or at least cheaply) available via the cloud.

## SaaS FOR PATRONS

This brings up a point for public libraries—your patrons don't always have the means to purchase and outfit a computer of their own, so they come to you to for those services. While libraries can offer access to some software—Microsoft Office isn't that expensive for many libraries—not all software is available to us in the quantities necessary to make it available to our patrons. Very expensive software like Photoshop or some of Adobe's graphical design and publishing software can be prohibitive if we are looking at putting one copy on one computer. Trying to put several copies on several patron computers is completely out of reach for most libraries. Becoming familiar with cloud-based alternatives for popular—and expensive—software packages and providing your patrons with links to those alternatives can be a valuable service you provide to your patrons. A list of current alternatives to various software packages is in chapter 14 of this book, but, because of the nature of the web and the speed at which things change, that list may be outdated by the time you read this. If so, don't give up—use your network (mailing lists, forums, conferences, etc.) to find out what other libraries are using in the place of traditional software and offer that to your patrons instead.

While the benefits for patrons who can't afford their own computers are clear—the ability to access software at no cost to them and in a way that is easily transferable from one computer to another—there are many benefits for libraries that use cloud-based software, too. One benefit is one that has popped up repeatedly in the various chapters of this book: SaaS can be much easier on the budget than traditional software packages. The ability to rent software, as opposed to buying it, can bring some substantial budgetary benefits. Often the cost of the software plus the cost of any maintenance fees plus the cost of the hardware on which that software can run add up to more than the cost of renting software that can run on just about any computer that can run a browser. SaaS does not require a workhorse of a machine to run it, generally. Most SaaS offerings are accessed through the browser and require only enough horsepower to run that browser. Another benefit is the lack of interaction required for updates and bug fixes. For traditionally installed software, your organization has to have a fairly regular schedule of updates and patches in order to keep the software running smoothly and securely on your computers. Software that is not patched and updated can be a big hole through which hackers can get into your network. SaaS software lessens that risk and makes the actual task of updating, patching, and upgrading a responsibility of the vendor, not your library. Other benefits include better support; many vendors of SaaS have their own support forums and provide support themselves for their customers. Other vendors have enthusiastic and helpful communities that have sprung up around their free services and that function as software support when it is needed. One last benefit that I will touch on here is the ability to get up and running very quickly with an SaaS solution. Often the length of time required for a traditional software installation is considerably longer than that of an SaaS service. For a traditional software installation, the usual process is to check that your computers and/or network can actually run the software, create a test installation to make sure it will work, determine the number of licenses needed, and then order the software and go through the process of installing it on every client (if necessary) or on the server that you've provisioned for it. For an SaaS project, you can skip the installation part altogether; the chances are every computer you own already has the necessary browser installed to access the software. The testing process can be considerably shortened as well; just a week's or month's demonstration account and assigning a couple of people to use that demo account will suffice for most SaaS services. Hard-core computer compatibility and making sure that the client will run on your computers are no longer necessary.

The drawbacks to using the cloud for SaaS services are also pretty standard: the lack of control, the need for more bandwidth to handle the increased traffic across your network, and the fact that you don't actually own the software. One of the drawbacks to SaaS is vendor lock-in. If you choose a particular vendor for your HR software needs, for example, it's a good idea to make sure that vendor uses open and industry-approved data formats. If you decide to move to a different provider later, without those open data formats, you may end up being unable to get your data from your old vendor to your new vendor. This is an important part of the evaluation process for any cloud-based software, but is especially important for business-critical software that manages important activities like payroll.

The software types profiled in this chapter are useful for the business side of running a library, but they are not the only options you have in the SaaS arena. Every type of software—from business-class productivity software to games to educational software—is becoming available in a cloud-based service. If it's not available yet, just wait a bit and try to search again; someone will write something that you can use!

## iEMPLOYEE AND OTHER HR SERVICES

Libraries have to manage the same kind of human resources requirements that any other employer has to manage. In doing this online, your organization has another opportunity to off-load HR expertise and use the cloud to supplement your library's skills without hiring another person or spending a great deal of money. Because HR functions are business functions and businesses rarely get things for free, all of the time sheet/HR software packages I have seen in the past cost money—whether they are cloud-based or not. The cloud-based ones, however, tend to cost less money over time and provide more features for that money, again because of the economies of scale that cloud-based software can provide.

One vendor of HR services for libraries is iEmployee (http://www. asuresoftware.com/products/asureforce). It's one of the examples of cloud-based software that is useful and usable by libraries. iEmployee is a cloud-based time sheet and attendance software package that libraries can use to manage benefit accruals such as time off and vacations and to manage hours worked by employees. As with most cloud-based software, you can pick and choose between various packages that include features and price points that work for your organization. The benefit of something like iEmployee for libraries is the flexibility it offers—if the library is closed for an unexpected snow day, the director can get into the time sheet software via any computer with Internet access and indicate it is a paid day off for scheduled staff that day. This reduces the work waiting when the library reopens and makes for a more flexible workplace when people can access their work from home with little difficulty.

Some of the features that iEmployee (and other SaaS packages in this field) can offer are:

- both employee and manager "self-service"—the ability for employees to enter their time and managers to look at it without organizational assistance;
- payroll provider integration—the ability to connect iEmployee (using APIs) to another company's payroll software easily;
- automated rules, customized for your organization—the cloud-based HR software can be customized for your particular benefit accrual schedule, among other things;
- centralized management—all the information is stored on that centralized server in the cloud, so the information is always in one spot, not spread among several different computers and file folders, as it often is with less centralized software packages;
- reporting features—many cloud-based software solutions offer ways to pull out data that are both easy and customizable; and
- security—most cloud-based HR solutions will offer excellent security features because the data is traveling over the open Internet between your building and the cloud.

## DESK STATS FOR REFERENCE

There are several statistical packages available for counting things such as questions asked at a reference desk—from a pen-and-paper chart on the desk to pretty sophisticated software that calculates averages and busy times and provides pretty reports. Some of those packages may even be available in a cloud-based, hosted version—or if they aren't now, they probably will be soon. Here, however, I'm going to focus on a single option that is cloud-based and free and has a great deal of support offered in the form of other librarians who are using the same system.

In the October 2011 issue of *Computers in Libraries*, Sunshine Carter and Thomas Ambrosi wrote an article detailing just how to create a reference desk statistics counter using the free tools available in Google Docs. That article is available online at http://www.infotoday.com/cilmag/oct11/Carter_

Ambrosi.shtml and takes the reader step-by-step through the process of creating a Google account (if you don't already have one), setting up a spreadsheet in the Google Docs (now Drive) applications, creating a form that will feed into that spreadsheet, and then publishing that form to a spot on the Internet where the reference desk folks can access it and update their question statistics in real time. All this is done with a cloud-based tool that can be accessed for free from any computer connected to the Internet.

This gives your reference staff the ability to infinitely customize your desk stats information—you choose what questions to ask, how to break those questions up, and how to organize the information. Someone with basic Excel skills can then download the spreadsheet each week or month and use the powerful reporting capabilities of Excel or OpenOffice Calc to present those statistics in charts or tables or as part of a narrative—whichever you feel is most needed in your library.

## CODE EDITORS

Code editing isn't just for programming geeks. Many librarians are being asked to update and maintain the library's website or to learn JavaScript to make that website have certain features. If this ever happens to you, you have cloud-based options as well. One option for cloud-based code editing is https://codeanywhere.net/. Others can be cobbled together using plain text editors and a service such as Dropbox or SugarSync (see chapter 7 of this book for more information about cloud-based file storage), but this is a native application and web-based option that will work on a bunch of different platforms without a lot of fussing from the coder.

Codeanywhere is both a website that you can access from any computer with an Internet connection and an app that works on iOS, Android, and in-browser (such as Chrome) platforms. It provides FTP access to a server, code syntax highlighting for a number of different languages, and help for just as

File   Edit   View   Insert   Format   Data   Tools   Form   Help      All changes saved in Drive

| | A | B | C | D | E | F | G |
|---|---|---|---|---|---|---|---|
| 1 | Timestamp | Query Source | Type of Query | | Query - What Reference Question Was Asked | Length of Interaction | |
| 2 | 4/1/2013 9:13:41 | Phone | Circulation | | Renewing Books | 2 | |
| 3 | 4/1/2013 9:14:03 | Walk-In | Reference | | Capital of Tibet | 4 | |
| 4 | | | | | | | |

**Figure 6.1.   An example of the spreadsheet in use in the desk stats software from the *Computers in Libraries* article.**

## Home

### Desk Statistics Tracker

\* Required

**Query Source** \*

○ Phone
○ Walk-In
○ Email
○ Text or Chat

**Type of Query** \*

○ Directional
○ Circulation
○ Reference
○ Computer

**Query - What Reference Question Was Asked**

**Figure 6.2.   An example of the form that collects the information that is displayed on the spreadsheet above.**

many different languages. It also provides a way for über-connected coding librarians to work while waiting in line at the bank or DMV—any phone, tablet, or laptop will run this software. There are options for both free and fee-based access; with fee-based access you will get more storage space for code and a "sandbox" that allows you to upload and test your web-based code in a browser. The free version, however, is perfectly usable for a coder who just needs to be able to do some work from somewhere other than in front of his or her workstation.

These examples—the iEmployee software, the do-it-yourself desk stats package, and the Codeanywhere application/browser-based code editor—are just the tip of the iceberg when it comes to non-library-specific miscellaneous software that is available in the cloud. Other types of software that aren't specifically library-related—e-mail, project management, social media, and graphical software to name but a few—will be covered in later chapters in this book. Here, however, I wanted to give you the impression that if you have a software need, the chances of it being fulfilled by a cloud-based product are pretty good. Use your favorite search engine to quickly find options for any "software in the cloud" need and then use the tips in this book and your network of librarian colleagues to determine the right service for you.

When evaluating SaaS solutions, consider the length of time the vendor has been in business and how much you are paying for the service. Just as this book was being finished, Xeround, a cloud Database as a Service (DaaS) provider, was announcing that they were going to be discontinuing their cloud database business and gave their paid customers two weeks' notice and their free customers a week's notice. This sort of quick cancellation of service is all too common in today's volatile cloud marketplace. This underscores the importance of asking questions like:

- How long have you been in business?
- What are your company's future plans?
- How can I get my data out of your service? Is it in a standard format? Is it easy to do?
- What kind of guarantees can you offer about notifications if you do stop doing business with us?

Most of all, being able to remove your data and import it into a competitor's product is crucial. It's the foundation of avoiding vendor lock-in and something you should insist upon with any vendor who will be storing or manipulating important data for you. Once you have some idea of the stability of the business and assurances from both the company and current (and past, if you can find them) customers that the data is removable, making a bet on a cloud provider can be a much less risky proposition.

One way to avoid finding yourself in this position is to consider open source. Choosing a vendor that uses an open-source platform can help keep you from finding yourself being dropped by a cloud provider who doesn't want to continue supporting the service. An open-source solution will be supportable by anyone who writes code and can pick up the mantle of support for that platform. This won't guarantee that you'll be able to find someone to do this, but it does increase the odds and it makes open-source-based cloud platforms very attractive.

*Chapter Seven*

# Manage Computers from the Cloud

One thing that most every library does these days is offer some kind of computing resources to their patrons. Depending on the size of the library and the library's service area, those resources could span from a single computer that doubles as an OPAC and patron workstation to a full-fledged computer lab with multiple computers and a full-time service desk devoted to the care and upkeep of those computers. Whatever the size of the service, there are certain things that will come up as your patrons use those computers—from ways to store documents, to software that patrons can use that is truly portable to other computers, to ways to prevent patrons from overstaying their welcome, to ways to remotely control a computer in the event that you can't physically get to it—controlling and/or managing a computer in a cost-effective way is a necessity for most public computer center administrators.

## FILE STORAGE

The nature of public computing means that file storage on the actual machine itself is problematic. Even if the hard drive were big enough to store all the documents from all of the patrons who use it, you are limiting patrons to using particular computers and making the sign-up and waiting list process for multiple computers a nightmare—determining which patron gets what computer becomes really difficult when you add that layer of requirement into the computer assignment service. Most libraries prefer completely identical computers to avoid patrons insisting on using one computer over another and causing these kinds of logistical problems. Allowing local document storage undoes all that work of making sure the computers are equal and alike. There are hardware solutions even after the demise of the floppy disk—flash USB drives are becoming quite cheap and some patrons have the means to cart around their own portable hard drives. No matter how cheap USB or other types of drives are, however, that is a barrier to use for some people, and it means that they may not be able to afford to save a document, such as a résumé, that may take more than one session on the computer to completely fill out. Cloud-based file storage can provide free online access to those stored documents without the need to use any particular computer—even a library computer—and without the need to spend money on an easily lost hardware device.

One of the most popular consumer-level file storage services is Google Drive (http://drive.google.com). Since everyone who has a Gmail account automatically has several gigabytes of space in a cloud-based drive (5GB at the time this book was written), it's usually the easiest one to get patrons to use when they want to store documents between sessions on your computers. Google Drive used to be known as Google Docs and, unlike some file storage options, has the ability to edit certain file types in the cloud as well. This is why you will see Google Drive listed under both the file storage and the end-user software section below. For our purposes in this section, however, Google Drive is just a very convenient way to store any document or file of any format online. For patrons with a Gmail account—and creating one with a patron is both easy and free—all that is required is to click on the Drive menu item in the black Google bar and then click on the upload button in the next screen. Once uploaded, that file is available to be downloaded to any computer with Internet access.

Another very popular file storage service is Dropbox (http://www.dropbox.com). The storage available through Dropbox starts out smaller than the other services—2GB for free—but can be expanded through various means, including signing other people up for free accounts or hooking up other services to your Dropbox account. The limit, if you choose to do those things, is up to 18GB of space for free. Dropbox is intended to sync files across computers by the installation of a small client that sets a "sync" folder on each computer and keeps that folder exactly the same as another "sync" folder on another computer. This is handy if you'd like to have documents available to either a work or home computer. It can also be useful as a backup solution for home use. For a computer center, however, you would skip the download and convenience of the client and use Dropbox just like Google Drive—as a website that allows you to upload and download documents and files to be saved in the cloud. There are no editing tools on the website, unlike Google Drive, but if you have editing software (MS Office, OpenOffice, etc.) on your public computers, your patrons can download a file, edit it, and upload it back to their Dropbox when they are done.

SugarSync (http://www.sugarsync.com) is very similar to Dropbox, though it does offer 5GB of space right off the bat for the free version and

ool (http://www.lanschool.com/) is a cloud-based classroom man-
olution. It is very usable for public computer labs that need to be
otrol computers remotely for all the reasons mentioned above and
e. It's not free but does offer a free trial, so you can decide if it's
ithout having to install server software or do more than sign up for
ther lab management solutions can be made to work with private
installing them on a local server and using them that way—those
signed to work through the browser are excellent candidates for
private cloud. The caveat for these kinds of software, though, is
them that use Windows will cost something to use—at least those
ar with do. You can get classroom lab software for free only if you
ux-based PC lab (which some libraries are heading toward as a
g measure anyway).

need, as they make use of public computer labs, many different
oftware. Testing, purchasing, installing, and maintaining that soft-
be difficult and expensive. Cloud-based software can help ease
ose costs and maintenance headaches associated with traditional
nd can give your IT department a break with updating and patch-
re installed on your library's computers. Even if you do offer all
nd whistles—Microsoft Office, Photoshop, and so on—making
are that other options such as Google Drive, Zoho, and Sumopaint
only be helpful for them and can make your patrons aware of the
hey can use when they are not able to use yours. Make use of the
I've provided in chapter 14 to help you make links to various
r your patrons—many patrons will find it useful to know about
s!

aditional software has—or will soon have—cloud-based alterna-
your favorite search engine or a handy reference librarian to find
urces and make them available to your patrons, either by directly
them as resources they can use on your computers or by creating
vith links, explanations, and recommendations from your staff. If
ndouts, though, be sure to check them regularly—things change
the Internet.

has more features for those who want to use it as a backup solution at home. For public computer lab purposes, however, it is another easy-to-use way to store, upload, and download files from the cloud for patrons who don't have any other way of storing files. It also lacks the in-place editing options of the Google Drive service, but it has a number of features that might make it attractive to many of your patrons, including specialized storage options for music and photos and specialized features for backing up a home computer.

There are other options—Box.net (http://www.box.net) and Skydrive (http://skydrive.live.com) are two of the bigger ones—but the three I've discussed here in this chapter are most likely to provide all the services your patrons will need, plus some. This is a growing market and there will also likely be other options available to you by the time you are reading this book that were not yet available when I was writing it. Again, check with your peers in similar library situations and see what they use—make use of conferences and mailing lists to ask questions and find new tools for you to offer to your patrons.

## END-USER SOFTWARE

End-user software is consumer software—office productivity suites, basic graphics packages, and so forth—that your patrons expect to be installed on your public computer lab machines for them to use. Most software packages, at least the commercially popular ones like Microsoft Office and Photoshop, are expensive—too expensive for most libraries to afford to put on every computer they offer to the public. This is where cloud-based alternatives come in. By offering links to these free, cloud-based software packages, you are offering your patrons the same benefits of cloud-based software that I laid out for libraries in chapter 6. While the features you get with cloud graphical editors may not compare with the features you get with a professional-level software package like Photoshop, they are pretty close to the sort of features you would get with the consumer-level Photoshop Elements, but at a price point of free, as opposed to $100 a copy. It is the same with office productivity software, too—you may not get every feature that Microsoft Word or PowerPoint provides, but you will get enough of them that the vast majority of your patrons will be happy.

The biggest cloud-based suite of consumer-level software is Google. Between Google Docs (http://drive.google.com—also known as Google Drive—see the file storage section at the beginning of this chapter for information on that) and Picasa, Google's image-editing and storage service, you can give your patrons access to word-processing, spreadsheet, and presentation software as well as graphical editing software. All of this is available for free in the cloud with a Google account. Patrons who choose to trade some information about themselves in return for access to all of this software will be able to write letters and résumés, use spreadsheets to manage numerical data, and create presentation slides for any type of presentation. Using Picasa (which is built into Google+ as the photo service), they can upload, edit, and insert images into those documents pretty easily, too.

If handing over their information to Google is something your patrons might not want to do, Zoho Office is another option for office suite productivity (http://www.zoho.com/). The free version of Zoho includes a number of business, collaboration, and productivity applications. The productivity applications are the ones that most patrons will be interested in and they include:

- Calendar;
- Notebook;
- Writer (word processing);
- Sheet (spreadsheet); and
- Show (presentation).

As with Google Docs, the benefit of this is that no software has to be installed and the documents and files that patrons create on your computers can be stored in the cloud and then accessed from any other computer with Internet access—whether or not that computer has software installed that can read that particular file format. This makes working at the local public library completely possible no matter what office suite software the library has installed, if any, and helps the library in supporting local small businesses and patrons who don't have the resources to do this sort of work themselves.

An example of the cloud-based graphical editors that are available is Sumopaint (http://www.sumopaint.com/app/). It offers, for the free version, a full-featured set of tools that would look very familiar to any user of Photoshop. There are paid versions that offer access to more filters and, for the most expensive option ($20 at the time of this writing), a desktop client that can be installed and used without an Internet connection. For the cloud version, however, no payment is needed and very sophisticated editing can happen with just a modern browser and some artistic talent. While there are many free options for graphical editing, the ability to edit on a computer that they don't own and can't install software on could be a real benefit for a lot of patrons. Even if you offer access to a more traditional desktop editor as well, pointing to a cloud-based one like Sumopaint is something that can educate your patrons for when they are using other people's computers outside of your library.

## TIME AND PRINT MANAGEMI

As of right now, traditional computer lab time as Envisionware, SAM, or Cassie—is installe tionally, through a client on a single comp change—perhaps by the time you are reading t traditional vendors will have released a cloud ware—right now, the choices for cloud-based tir few. One of those choices, Userful (http://www ample of a cloud-based time management soluti board" is accessed via a web browser, which anywhere, and since the product will work on th software package can be managed with very lit ment needed.

As with most cloud-based solutions, this is h be useful for a number of situations, from very computers to a small library with just one or two of the pay structure is pay for what you use and i can have the benefits of full-featured and wel packages without having to pay big prices. Userfi will undoubtedly be joined by other cloud time a ware in the future.

Another new time management application tha cloud-based system is Libki (http://libki.org/), a source time and management system. Since it i server can be placed anywhere on the Internet, m cloud-based software package as well. Libki, be source, might be a good solution for very small budgets or for very large libraries or library conso the software between multiple locations without server to manage it all within each branch or locatio

## LAB MANAGEMENT

One thing that many libraries appreciate is the at their public computers. From a safety perspective, i down a computer to help convince an angry patr having to physically approach the computer. It's als a password—to bypass a filter or get a patron in library resource like the local newspaper—without word on the keyboard in front of the patron. For tl remote control software installation is handy to have

Lansc agement able to c many m worth it a demo. clouds b that are use witl that any I'm fam have a cost-sa\

Patr types c ware c some c softwa ing so the be patron exist c resour resour servic these

M tives. those linkir hand you quic

*Chapter Eight*

# E-mail in the Cloud

Most people these days use, in some way, cloud-based e-mail. Those who exclusively use a client such as Outlook, Outlook Express, or Thunderbird with e-mail managed through an in-house server are becoming a rare breed. Most people have at least a "throwaway" address that they use for signing up to new services and contests and other low-value applications that is provided by Yahoo!, Hotmail (Microsoft), or Google, if not one of a number of other cloud-based mail options. While you can use a desktop client to access cloud-based e-mail, generally it is accessed via the web browser or through a specialized app on a mobile device. With the exception of some businesses, even people who use the industry standard Exchange e-mail from Microsoft are beginning to use the cloud-based, rented solution instead of dealing with the hassles of managing an e-mail server themselves.

There is no denying—managing an e-mail service can be a full-time job in and of itself. E-mail is a very popular vector for bad guys to get into a network, so the person managing the e-mail must be very security conscious. It's also considered a critical business function for many businesses—much of the work that happens these days uses e-mail as the communication medium; when it goes down, work stops, so the person managing the e-mail must be good at keeping servers up and running with very little downtime. E-mail is also plagued with the problem of spam—enough junk e-mail gets sent that it can constitute a fair amount of the total traffic on any given network, so the person managing the e-mail must be a filtering and spam-fighting expert as well. While you can find these kinds of people with these kinds of skills, they are not cheap. The best way to manage e-mail these days is to pick a cloud vendor and let them handle the issues of security, spam filtering, and server wrangling to keep your important e-mail conversations flowing.

## GOOGLE APPs FOR DOMAINS

Google's e-mail service—Gmail (http://www.gmail.com)—comes bundled with a number of other services and has a good deal of "extra" stuff along with it. The basics, though, are a 25G e-mail inbox (for $50 per year per user) with integrated Calendar, Document, and file storage and IM capabilities built in. Gmail also has a Task application that is pretty well integrated into the e-mail as well as many other services that are more or less integrated with the e-mail service. Part of what makes Gmail so attractive is the ability to log into a single service (e-mail, for example) and have access to numerous other services using the same credentials. As with all of the cloud e-mail providers mentioned in this section, Gmail also allows organizations to use their own domain names for their e-mail—so your e-mail addresses can be *user@organization.org* instead of *user@gmail.com*. This makes Gmail perfectly suitable for business class e-mail.

A unique benefit to Gmail is the Lab feature. This gives end users a great deal of control over the look and functionality of their e-mail. The Labs are small applications that work with Gmail's e-mail in some way—either by rearranging the inbox page or by changing the way you send your e-mails. These are user-configurable, meaning that an administrator is not necessary to make them work—users can go to their settings and turn on or off any of the Lab applications they want to use or not use.

The Google Apps Dashboard—the way Gmail is administered in an organization like a library, as opposed to a single e-mail address—gives administrators a way to make sure that all e-mail addresses, groups, and lists are run properly through a centralized administration panel. Through this panel, new e-mails and groups can be created, reports on e-mail usage viewed, and extra marketplace services added and deleted. Administrators can decide whether their users get the latest Gmail upgrades immediately or whether they wait until the admins can try them out and create training materials for them first, which is a huge help for bigger organizations who want to be sure all training is done before the features are rolled out. Administrators can also tweak the way groups and mailing lists are created and managed through the Dashboard, as well as how users are arranged and managed through the use of organizational units and their individual administrators.


## MSN

Microsoft's Exchange Mail Server is a standard among business-class e-mail providers. For many years it has been available to anyone who can install the software on a server and configure and administer it (after purchasing the sometimes quite expensive software for the server and the client first, of

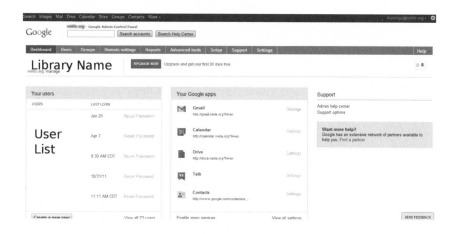

**Figure 8.1.    The dashboard interface for Google Apps.**

course), something that often required formal classroom training to be able to do well. Microsoft does, however, offer a cloud-based version that gives you the functionality of the Exchange Server with the convenience of vendor-managed cloud hosting.

The hosted Exchange service is part of Microsoft's Office 365 product. The mail-only portion is, as of this writing, $48 per year per user, but does not include access to the Office software online portion for that price. To get the full features of Office 365, you must pay for both for a minimum price of $240 per user per year (for the Professional Version, the only one available for purchase at the time this book was being written—http://www.microsoft.com/en-us/office365/compare-plans.aspx). This is quite a bit more than what you would pay for Gmail's Apps, but it does give you online, cloud-based access to all of Microsoft Office Suite's programs, as well as 25GB of e-mail space with unlimited e-mail storage. It includes some PBX and voicemail services, but those seem to be pretty comparable to Google Voice, which can be integrated into Google Apps.

The biggest benefit to using Office 365 is the access to online versions of the exact same programs you use on your organization's computers now—Microsoft Word, Excel, PowerPoint, Outlook, and more. While both Google and Zoho have compatible applications, they aren't 100 percent the same as Microsoft's applications—and for many staff members and public computer center users, that will cause some confusion and can make performing basic tasks harder for a while, until the new interface is learned.

MS Office 365 also has an administrator's dashboard that gives the e-mail admin a way to manage e-mail addresses, mailing lists and groups, and much more. It very much simplifies the administration of the Exchange e-mail service, as compared to managing a full-blown server. You can also access tech support through the dashboard if you find it necessary.

## Zoho

Zoho offers a mail-only cloud-hosted solution (that does include a calendar, tasks, and a notes application as well, but not full office productivity applications, like Google Apps and MS 365—http://www.zoho.com/mail/) that gives you 10GB of space for $24 per user per year or 15GB of space for $36 per user per year. You can add the same sort of productivity software you get from Google Apps (word processor, spreadsheet, presentation software) for $3 or $5 more per user per year. Still more applications can be added on as well, for fairly reasonable prices for smaller organizations.

As with Google and Microsoft, Zoho supports custom domains and a free trial to see if their solution will work for you. This service is a bit less well-known than either Google Apps or Microsoft Office, so it may be well worth doing the thirty-day trial to see if it will work for your organization before you choose a cloud-based solution for your library.

Also like Google and Microsoft, Zoho has an administrative dashboard that lets you administer both the e-mail and the other services that have been added onto your domain. From this dashboard you can also add and remove services as needed without worrying about installing or uninstalling programs and features from a server. As with the previous two services, the dashboard in Zoho Mail makes e-mail management much more accessible to IT without requiring specialized e-mail management skills.

While each of these e-mail solutions has its pros and cons, they are all cloud-based and ready for you to try out for a bit before you make a final decision. Both Google Apps and Microsoft Office 365 offer direct access to tech support for their products; Zoho seems to be the only one that doesn't offer that—though it's also the least expensive of the three, so that is not a big surprise. All three offer trial versions that are easy to set up and use—no client software beyond a browser is required to make use of these services.

The things to really look out for in the e-mail space are the ability to stop spam, or at least reduce it to a trickle as opposed to a flood; the ability to access e-mail from the web or from mobile devices of pretty much any kind; and the "uptime" factor. Spam reduction is where Google's Gmail really shines—they have put some serious effort into the spam-catching features of their e-mail service and it shows. Microsoft and Zoho also have spam-filtering services, but Gmail is known for its ability to catch spam without catching too many nonspammy e-mails as well. All three of the e-mail services mentioned in this chapter have web interfaces that will work on any device—mobile or not—that has access to the Internet, and all of them have native

**Figure 8.2.    The dashboard for the Zoho mail and applications product.**

mobile apps as well. If you choose to go with a different cloud e-mail service, ask them what devices they support. At the very least you will want to have web, Android, and iOS support, though more is better! Finally, the amount of uptime (time spent up and working between failures) is critical for e-mail services. Failures happen—to everyone and every service. The cost of providing 100 percent uptime would be extremely prohibitive, so the trick here is to decide both how much uptime you can afford to buy and how much downtime you can afford to lose in your work. Most libraries will tend toward less expensive services with lower uptime rates, but some might consider e-mail to be so crucial to their work that they end up being willing to pay more for more guaranteed uptime.

Uptime, in the technical world, is measured in 9's—as in 99.999% guaranteed uptime for a particular service. That is five 9's and is a gold standard for cloud-based services. A five 9's guarantee of uptime means that your service will be down for no more than five minutes over the course of a year. That sort of guarantee is expensive. Most cloud vendors offer in the range of two to three 9's (99 to 99.9%), which comes out to between eight hours and three days of downtime a year. Google Apps for Business, at the time of this writing, had a 99.9% uptime guarantee, meaning that if your Google Apps service is down for more than eight hours a year, they will reimburse you some prorated amount of money in return.

Most organizations these days use some version of Microsoft Office Suite to provide word-processing, spreadsheet, e-mail client, and other programs that are useful in day-to-day business, but those programs can be expensive if you are providing them for a number of different computers, and even more expensive if you are providing them for the public as well. Looking into a cloud-based vendor like Google, Zoho, or Microsoft's own solution can be less expensive than purchasing, installing, patching, updating, and upgrading a client-based solution on every computer in your organization.

*Chapter Nine*

# Project Management

Project management (PM) is one of those topics that can—and does—fill entire bookshelves. Getting into the hows and whys of using PM tools and techniques is beyond the scope of this book, but some good starter references for those who are interested in PM include:

- the Project Management Institute (the certification body of the PM profession)—http://www.pmi.org;
- the Project Management Hut—articles on PM—http://www.pmhut.com; and
- Project Management Think—articles and resources for project managers—http://www.pmthink.com.

PM does have a full professional certification and a book that encapsulates the "body of knowledge" for the profession. If you would like to learn what the certification process will cover, you can check out *A Guide to the Project Management Body of Knowledge (PMBOK Guide)*, which is published by the Project Management Institute; the most recent version (as of this writing) was published on January 1, 2013, but it will probably be the most recent version for a few more years. While a certification in PM isn't at all necessary to use PM tools, such as the ones I'll cover below, it is a nice (though expensive) way to prove to employers that you have a solid knowledge of how to use the tools and processes in their work.

For those who are already using PM processes in their daily work, moving some of those processes to the cloud can be both time and frustration saving. Because PM activities—perhaps as much or more than any others detailed thus far in this book—are collaborative in the sense that many people have a need to at least see parts of the project plan and others have a need to be able to edit project materials, cloud-based tools are incredibly useful.

Traditional PM software—a locally installed copy of Microsoft Project, for example—is frequently used to manage projects from a single computer, using a single file and in the ultimate control of a single person. Project files can be shared, but not as easily or conveniently as with a cloud-based program. In today's collaborative environments, that is often an issue. Sharing MS Project files among several people is problematic as well. Keeping track of the latest version and who has what information can be a nightmare if you are doing it in the traditional manner by e-mailing project files back and forth to one another. Deciding on a cloud-based platform helps to alleviate those issues and brings a level of collaboration that is hard to match in traditional software.

The essential functions of a cloud-based PM system for more than one person should include:

- centralized file storage;
- communication functions built-in (e-mail or IM);
- calendar;
- scheduling resources (not just people); and
- budgeting.

Other functions that are nice to have in a good PM system would include:

- contact/human resources storage;
- templates;
- guidance on phases, processes, and workflows;
- Gantt and WBS (work breakdown structure) creators; and
- fine-grained reporting capabilities.

While some of the software that is available on the market now does actually fulfill all of these points, that software is generally enterprise-level software, with enterprise-level price tags. Some cobbling together of software, however, can get you nearly all of the above features for much less than the cost of a traditional software package.

In this chapter, I'll focus on a set of cloud-based or at least web-based software that you can use to replace much of the traditional PM software. Not all of it is free, but all of it is going to be accessible from the web and all of it will be easy to use with a team of people.

## Basecamp AND Tom's Planner

A collaborative work environment that also does a great job of being a PM tool, Basecamp (http://www.basecamp.com) is PM software that acts as a repository for files, ideas, contact information, and everything else that accumulates during the course of a project. The structure puts everything related to a project on a single page—all the discussions, to-do lists, and files are listed, giving you a nice overview of the entire project in one quick glance.

Much of the work of a project can be done through Basecamp—they have PM templates that help you pull together the parts of Basecamp that you need for certain types of projects—and you can edit, discuss, and finalize text and other project deliverables right in the Basecamp interface. A single contact list and calendar for everyone makes getting together face-to-face easier, too, recognizing that not all meetings are best done online.

Basecamp really shines in the area of communication. It is very easy to communicate with team members, stakeholders (those who have a vested interest in the project, whether or not they are actually working on it—funders, patrons, etc.), and others about the progress of the project. There are threaded discussion boards, built-in instant messaging tools, and much more that makes communication between all interested parties easy—and when it's easy, it's more likely to get done.

Reports—including a daily recap of the previous day's activities along with many others—are available, too. A "visual timeline" also helps the project manager in staying on top of the work being—or not being—done. All of this combines to provide easy documentation of every project, something that PM "best practices" definitely recommend.

As with many cloud-based services, Basecamp also takes care of back-end issues for you. Backups of all of your data are done nightly, and all upgrades and updates to all the various bits of software running a Basecamp site are done behind the scenes and without any attention from you or your IT department, should you have one.

Basecamp offers several levels of service for several levels of pricing. Some of them are fairly reasonable for smaller project teams, so one might be right for your organization. Basecamp, however, doesn't provide everything a project might need, so finding those tools online and in the cloud is helpful. One such tool is Tom's Planner.

Tom's Planner (http://www.tomsplanner.com) is an online Gantt chart creator. That's pretty much all it does, but since many of the PM packages that I've come across don't offer Gantt chart creation, if you really need to use one to help you organize your resources, Tom's Planner offers a free version that is pretty useful. As a matter of fact, you can begin a Gantt chart without ever signing up for an account at all, though if you want to save it to work on later, you'll need to sign up for the free account at least.

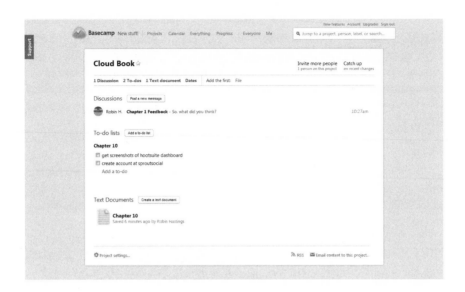

**Figure 9.1.   This is the single-page project view in Basecamp.**

The free account offers access to the Gantt chart software, but no printing, saving, or exporting features. For that you'll need to use the next level of service, which is, as of this writing, about $9 per month. That amount of money, though, gives you a lot more functionality. For basic, small projects for which only one or two people will ever need to refer to the Gantt chart, though, the personal account will likely be enough.

## OTHER PM TOOLS

Starting with Project Online (http://www.microsoft.com/project/en-us/preview/default.aspx), the cloud-hosted version of the traditional category leader MS Project, we can find a number of other PM tools as cloud-based options. Project Online is part of the Office Professional cloud version 2013 of the MS Suite. It is streamlined and easier to use than the clunky and feature-laden traditional software that it has grown out of, but it's pricey in comparison with some other tools. Of course, you get a full PM suite for that price, with Gantt chart creation and calendaring and full integration with SharePoint, if you have access to that software as well. For a Microsoft-heavy organization, moving MS Office to the cloud and using the online version of Project is a reasonable choice.

GroupCamp is another paid option for bigger organizations. For $24 a month (at the time of this writing) you can get fifteen projects, 4GB of

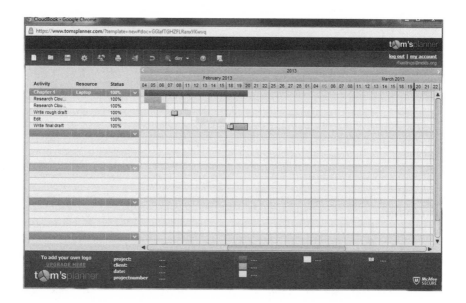

**Figure 9.2.   A Gantt chart created in Tom's Planner software.**

storage space, and unlimited users. That's the smallest plan available, though of course there is a thirty-day trial to give you a chance to decide if it contains the features you need for your organization's projects. GroupCamp contains a lot of reporting features—for managers who are keeping track of a lot of different projects using different resources (people, time, money, etc.), this might be the best choice.

While the similarities are clear, GroupCamp has a slightly different inter-face than the Basecamp industry standard. Everything is not on one page—there are tabs along the top that hold an activity list page, an overview page, a list of files, tasks, discussions, milestones, a time log, and a wiki (though you can add or subtract these options from your project's site). The milestones feature is interesting as it provides both a Gantt chart and list-based look at your upcoming "milestone" dates. This is something that Basecamp doesn't offer right out of the box and would keep you from having to make use of a separate Gantt chart software option like Tom's Planner. Everything in GroupCamp can be linked up—milestones to task lists, files to milestones, and people to discussions, if necessary. While this is a pricier option than Basecamp (by about $4 a month), it is a more complete PM solution.

Google fans have options, too! If you have Google Apps for Domains and want to add some PM functionality to your applications, there are several options in the Google Marketplace that can be useful for you. Do by Sales-force (bit.ly/WMOxld) is an option as is Gantter Project (bit.ly/Xwfwkk).

**Figure 9.3.    GroupCamp's Activity Page, the first page you see when you enter a project site.**

They are both free and both available through the Marketplace. Both offer PM tools that work across an entire GApps domain and templates to get you started on some common project types. Gantter also will work with MS Project files. For Agile PM shops, the Pivotal Tracker (bit.ly/WWoadI) is an option for agile management of projects that uses your existing Google Apps applications.

Other PM applications offer at least basic PM tools but are tuned to work with specific kinds of projects (see Jumpchart for web design projects or Trac Project for code-based programming projects). These include:

- Lighthouse—http://www.lighthouseapp.com (paid, can integrate with a subversion code repository for code-based projects);
- Springloops—http://www.springloops.com (free or paid options, also integrates with subversion code repository);
- CreativePro Office—http://www.mycpohq.com (paid, includes office productivity software online, as well as PM tools);
- Jumpchart—http://www.jumpchart.com (free or paid options, more web design project software than general PM software); and
- Trac Project—http://trac.edgewall.org (open source and wiki based, includes interfaces to many version control code repositories such as subversion and includes bug tracking).

There are many other options for cloud-based PM tools both free and for a fee. Just about any tool that is web-based is going to work as a cloud-based option for your organization. Because of the collaborative nature of most projects, using a cloud, or at least web-based, tool is smart.

Project work is done using a variety of tools, some cloud-based, some not, during the course of the project. The actual work of planning and managing the project, though, can be done entirely online, with cloud-based software and in a collaborative way that encourages the kind of communication that is necessary for a project to succeed.

The list of features above gives a good overview of the kinds of features that you will want to look for in a PM solution. If your organization works on a few small projects throughout the year, one of the free versions of the listed software will do nicely in order to get everyone on the same page and keep everyone on track. If you are planning a huge project in the future, however—a building project or a major service addition—you may want to invest in a full-featured PM service like MS Project Online or GroupCamp/Basecamp. These are more expensive options, but they include many of the features that make managing a large project (or even many littler projects) easy. The more you can stick to the processes and activities of a formal PM, as you can with most of the services detailed in this chapter, the more successful your future projects may be.

*Chapter Ten*

# Social Media in the Cloud

Using social media is nearly a requirement for modern libraries. Our patrons are present in that arena, discussing what they want and need, and only by being there ourselves can we be sure we are filling those wants and needs. Social media is becoming another marketing tool for libraries as well—it's a relatively cheap way to let a lot of people know what we are doing and when we are doing it. The ability to both broadcast our events and news and carry on personal and one-on-one conversations through the same medium is invaluable for libraries with limited marketing funds available. However you decide to do your social media, though, the chances are that you can use some form of cloud-based service to help you out. Between alert services that give you material with which you can populate your social media accounts and ways to cut the amount of work required to keep a social media campaign going strong over time, using the cloud to help connect your organization to your patrons is something that will increase the value of the time you invest in a social media campaign.

Social media management encompasses both the ability to scan and pull out the relevant posts in any given social network but also the ability to post (and repost, if necessary) at the right times to catch the right people.

## ALERTS

Why use an alert system as part of your social media strategy? Because your patrons, the people who use your service—as well as people in your service area who don't use your services—are talking about you. At the very least, they are talking about the kinds of service you provide, as a library, and you need to be a part of that conversation. When someone complains about your library online, the best thing you can do is engage them personally to find out what went wrong. Sometimes, it is just a matter of education—one Tweet complaining about a library at which I worked ended up being resolved quite easily when the patron was educated about our interlibrary loan service and a request was put in on her behalf. She ended the transaction with an entirely different outlook on the library (which she also Tweeted without any prompting on the library's part) and is now much more empowered to make use of the kinds of services libraries in general can provide. Not all complaints will be that easy to confront and resolve, but many really will.

Other things you might "hear" from your patrons are wishes for services that you provide—someone who really needs to be able to access a journal article but doesn't want to pay the money to do so needs to hear from you that you have the full text article available at your library and that you will help them get it for free. Someone who lives in your area and wishes there were a "Netflix-like service for books" that would let them just download books to their reader needs to hear about your e-book service(s) and how they can access them. Without a concentrated effort to listen and respond, however, those kinds of opportunities to repair your image, engage your patrons, and educate your service area will be lost.

One alert service is provided by a familiar company—Google (http://www.google.com/alerts). The service offers alerts that can be sent directly to your inbox (see below) in your e-mail or subscribed to as an RSS feed in your favorite RSS reader. Setting up an alert is just a matter of performing a search in Google (from the alerts page given above) and, if the results you get back are acceptable, subscribing to that search. Google will run that search for you on a regular basis—daily or weekly as you choose—and send you the new results each time the search is run. In the image below, I have set up an alert for any mention of libraries on the web or as a blog search, so anytime someone mentions libraries, the article or blog post gets sent to my e-mail inbox.

Another alert service that is less well known is Social Mention (http://socialmention.com/). It also performs searches for whatever terms you enter, but it also includes social media in the results. Instead of just doing a web or blog search, you can search in blogs, microblogs (Twitter or Yammer or Identi.ca), comments, events, images, and more—so the searches you do can be more finely tailored to just what you need. Once the search is done, you can have the results e-mailed to you, subscribe to the RSS feed of the new results, or download the results in CSV format. What Social Mention provides that Google doesn't is an analysis of your search term; you can see how people feel about your term with a "sentiment" ratio (the ratio of positive to negative mentions of your search term on the social media sites that Social Mention searches) and get some idea of the reach of your term—how many people see the term in their social media networks. If you want to track what people are saying specifically about your organization in social networks

News                                    8 new results for **library OR libraries**

Golfers pull out clubs while at the **library**
Iowa City Press Citizen
The event marks one of the few times the **library** receives private sponsorship, as local businesses
supported each hole. Proceeds from the first event in in 2009 helped the **library** begin opening on
Sundays, while Coralville Public **Library** Foundation ...
See all stories on this topic »

Little Free **Libraries** spread across city, world
Milwaukee Journal Sentinel
Brooks' best estimate is more than 6,000 **libraries** in 36 countries, including 52 in Ghana and seven
in Pakistan. He suspects there are many more because not everyone registers their **library** at
littlefreelibrary.org. It's such a simple idea. Anyone can ...
See all stories on this topic »

Check it out: Public **libraries** have a new playbook
The Oshkosh Northwestern
Although some public **libraries** are offering unusual items for patrons to borrow to boost usage, the
Oshkosh Public **Library** is sticking with its core mission of boosting literacy, albeit branching out
with electronic books and other decidedly non ...
See all stories on this topic »

Little Free **Libraries** encourage reading
Record-Searchlight
Hosts decorate their **libraries** and will be responsible for maintaining them. Koppes said the book
stations aren't just for picture books and chapter books for children. Books that appeal to all ages are
welcome. "The idea is whatever the **library** would ...
See all stories on this topic »

Man arrested in Queens **library** sex assault
7Online.com
The incident happened around 6 p.m. last Monday in the Queens Public **Library** at 40-
20 Broadway in Astoria. Now, Hector Troche is charged with sex abuse, forcible
touching and public lewdness. Police say he approached the 15-year-old girl, grabbed          7Online.com
her ...
See all stories on this topic »

FRG **library** full of programs in March, April

**Figure 10.1. Google's Alert email—searching for library OR libraries on the
web.**

without having to search each one individually, Social Mention could be
valuable for you.

## Sprout Social

Sprout Social (http://sproutsocial.com/pricing) is a professional-grade social
media management package priced at $39 per month per user for ten ac-
counts. It provides engagement (tracking conversations), monitoring, publishing (including scheduled posts), and analytics (reports on usage) for that
money. For some organizations, having all of those functions in one spot and
with one interface can be worth the money. For other organizations, however, the free/freemium options (see HootSuite below combined with Google
Alerts above) can be just as useful when combined properly. Sprout Social
does offer a thirty-day trial so that you can get a chance to give it a test run
before deciding whether to pay for a social media manager that does nearly
everything under one roof.

## HootSuite

HootSuite is one of a growing number of "social media managers" that connects to several different social media accounts (Facebook, Twitter, a blog, etc.) and allows you to both monitor those accounts—see who is posting on them—and post to them. HootSuite is a freemium service—you get much of the functionality for free, but if you'd like to have more managers added to the account, or more social media accounts added, you will have to upgrade to a paid version. The free version, however, lets one manager manage up to five social media accounts.

The management of those accounts includes both keeping track of what your friends on those social networks are saying through the dashboard, but also posting timely information, even when you might not have time to do it right at the moment. HootSuite, along with several of the other social media managers on the market, allows you to schedule posts to Twitter or Facebook or wherever so that they can be posting while you are working on other things. Like scheduling posts in blogging, this allows you to create content when you have time and have it trickle out consistently from your various social accounts. The ability to schedule a post to appear on Facebook, Twitter, Pinterest, or any other social network you might use is invaluable—and the cloud-based services that allow it are incredibly useful. The ability to target posts—creating one for Facebook and another for Twitter, for example—is another benefit of using a social media manager like HootSuite. Using one that is cloud-based just makes the updating on a schedule part easier—you don't have to worry about a computer being on all the time or being accidentally turned off when the updates are supposed to go out.

When you first sign up for a HootSuite account, you get the opportunity to log into your existing social media accounts—the first options are Facebook, Twitter, Google+, LinkedIn, Foursquare, a Wordpress blog of your own, and Myspace. Once you've logged into whatever accounts you want to manage from HootSuite, you are taken to your home or dashboard page, where you see each account represented in a tab along the top. Clicking on the tab gives you columns of information—for Twitter the default columns are Friends, Mentions, and Direct Messages, so you can see what the people you follow are saying to the world and directly to you. You can add other columns, including a search column or two that lets you track mentions of your library or organization even by Tweeters you don't follow.

## WHAT TO TRACK

Once you have some alert accounts set up or you have Sprout Social or HootSuite set up and are ready to add tracking columns to their interfaces, you need to decide what it is you want to track. Generally, you will want to search on your name and variations thereof. If you are Main Street Public Library, you will want to do a search for "Main Street Public Library" *or* "MSPL" *or* "Your Town's Public Library" *or* any other name you might be known as. Don't forget to search on your domain name, the name of your director or PR person (if they do most of the media contacts), or on any other social network name you might be using (search for mentions of your Twitter handle, for example). You also want to track keywords like "journals" or "reading" or "homework" or whatever is on the minds of your local patrons to which you want to respond. Many tracking services allow you to limit results by location—HootSuite, for example, gives you the opportunity to append your location to your search query, limiting the results to Tweeters in your area.

Other things to look for include names of library supporters (or critics) in your area and news items that refer to the library or to your "competition"—find out what people are saying about your local bookstores or DVD rental places to get a handle on what you should be doing to market your books and DVDs. Keep track of the big conferences—ALA and other national-level conferences are good, but remember to track the state-level associations and local conferences, too. They may have good information for you that is cheaper and more local than the big conferences.

## HASHTAGS

One thing you must understand in order to do any of this tracking on Twitter (though they are being used on other social networks these days, too, including just recently becoming available on Facebook) is the hashtag. Hashtags are words or phrases that begin with a hash mark (#) and are used to tie together multiple Tweets or other posts into one big conversation. A hashtag like #ALA2013 can be used by everyone who attends the ALA conference in Chicago in the summer of 2013 to provide a way for all the Tweets about or from that conference to be grouped together. This provides functionality for attendees, since they can see what is being discussed and where fellow conferencegoers are at any given time, and it provides functionality for those who can't go and who are watching the conference from afar—they can follow that hashtag using Twitter or a social media alert service and see what people are talking about and learning and generally discussing while at the conference. Any social alert service will follow hashtags as will just about any social media management service. On Twitter, Facebook, or FriendFeed, those hashtags are clickable—when clicked upon, they start a search that combs through the public Tweets or posts, finding all instances of that hashtag. This makes keeping together a group of posts on a similar subject easy.

While this chapter has focused on new-media social media, there are times when the old-fashioned sort of media comes in handy. E-mail has been around for far longer than Twitter or Facebook or even Myspace and is in use pretty extensively with the older generations. To supplement your social media campaigns, you may want to look into a service such as MailChimp (http://www.mailchimp.com), which offers mailing list management through the cloud. For less than twelve thousand e-mails sent per month (at the time of this writing), the MailChimp service is free—and for a few dollars every now and then, you can get extras like an "Inbox Doctor" that looks over your e-mails and finds text or images that may trigger spam filters or otherwise keep your e-mails from people's inboxes. You can do A/B campaigns—send an e-mail to part of your mailing list with one subject while part of your list gets another to determine which subject line prompts the most opening clicks from your audience. MailChimp will compare the rates at which those mailings are opened and acted upon to give you some insight into what subjects do best. You can take that same A/B testing to HootSuite—send Tweets about the same subject with slightly different text and a different URL (use bit.ly to create unique URLs that can be tracked) and watch to see which ones get clicked the most.

Social media management can take up a whole book—much more can be done to ensure that your message gets out and is heard by the people who need to hear it. Here, however, we are focusing on the cloud-based services that help you in your social media endeavors. The sorts of things you want to look for in a cloud-based social media manager are the ability to search using sophisticated queries in order to get exactly the information you need, a dashboard that puts all of your accounts in one place so that with one login you can control multiple accounts for the same library, and the ability to schedule posts. The ability to test the efficiency of the posts you make is a plus, but the ability to schedule a post to come out when you are not in front of your computer is a must.

Keeping all that in mind, you can put together a pretty impressive suite of social media "helpers" for very little cost, or you can pay to have someone (see Sprout Social above) put together a selection of tools that will let you follow the conversation, join in on the conversation, and make sure your message is getting out there into other conversations. Marketing for libraries is all about conversations—we really aren't trying to sell anything; we just have to let people know that we are there and that we are ready and able to help them find what they need when they need it. That, of course, helps our cause when asking for more money from our tax base, but it's the reason we exist—and social media managers, combined with cloud technologies, really help libraries in getting their message across to their patrons.

*Chapter Eleven*

# Graphics in the Cloud

One of the things that has traditionally required a workhorse of a computer is high-end computer graphic creation. It still does, really, but if you want to just edit some existing artwork—photos or your logo or a scanned image— there are some pretty respectably powered options that require no more than a reasonably recent browser and a smidgen of artistic skill. Having some knowledge of file formats, filter options, and the limitations of browser-based image editing helps, though.

File formats are possibly the most important thing to understand about images on the web. There are a limited number of formats that web browsers understand without help—.jpg, .gif, and .png are the three most commonly used today; although .svg is commonly supported, it's not as commonly used. Nearly every one of the browser and/or cloud-based image editors you find will open and save files in those first three formats. If you work with professional graphic designers who have one of those high-end computer graphic stations, they may provide you with images or expect images from you that are in more traditional graphical formats. Beyond that, most graphical formats are pixel-based or raster formats. Some people, however, prefer to work in point-based or vector formats (such as SVG; see the SVG Edit program below for a more thorough discussion of raster versus vector graphics) because they never lose quality no matter how much you stretch them. Many logos are first created as vector images and then converted to web-friendly raster formats before being used on the web. Vector images are also well suited to printing because of the fact that they can be enlarged nearly to infinity without any of the pixel-based artifacts or blurriness associated with enlarging a raster image format.

While neither of the following programs are cloud-based and both require downloading and installing to a computer to be run locally, they are both very useful helpers to the cloud-based options I'm listing in this chapter. The first is a very capable graphical editor on its own. Gimpshop (http://www.gimpshop.com/) or the plain old GIMP 2 (http://www.gimp.org/) are versions of GIMP, a Photoshop clone that has come into its own and is now as useful (though maybe not as user-friendly) as the most current versions of Photoshop. These are desktop programs, but they are open source and free, so if you have graphical tasks that are beyond the capabilities of a graphical editor in a browser, those are good options for heavy-duty graphical editing.

## CLOUD-BASED GRAPHICAL EDITORS

One "full-service" image manipulation service is Pixlr (http://pixlr.com). It includes a standard editor, an "express" quick editor, a "Pixlr-o-matic" for fun filters and playful effects, as well as screen capture, image sharing, and mobile versions that all work through the browser, in the cloud with no downloads or special hardware required—just a computer that will run a fairly modern browser. As with the rest of the full-featured graphical editors in this section, the interface is very similar to the interface of Photoshop, the industry standard in graphical editing programs.

Pixlr, with its mobile version(s)—one for Android and one for iOS—is probably the most full-featured of the bunch. If you take a lot of photos at events and want to edit (crop, filter, touch up) them on the spot before uploading them to your Flickr account or Facebook page, the mobile versions of Pixlr let you do that easily. Pixlr also includes more than six hundred effects (for the mobile version—there are more for the regular version you use through your browser) and the ability to remove red-eye, whiten teeth, and resize any image with just a click or two.

Another of the graphical editors that are accessible through a browser is Splashup (http://www.splashup.com/). Splashup advertises easy photo storage using either its own image-sharing service or through Facebook, Picasa, or Flickr. Splashup also features layers and layer effects as well as multiple filters and brushes that work just like Photoshop's. Most of the features of Splashup are similar to Pixlr's and they are both free, so try them both out to see which one you like best.

Sumopaint (http://www.sumopaint.com/) is a bit different than the two previous graphical editors because it also includes a desktop version. You can download the Sumopaint desktop app if you choose the most expensive version of the software ($20 at the time of this writing). There is a free version, which includes the basics in cloud-based graphics; a medium-priced version ($9 at the time of this writing), which includes more filters and effects; and the most expensive version, which includes all that plus the

**Figure 11.1. Pixlr's open image screen.**

desktop app. If you need more power, you can pay the $20 and get a copy for your local machine as well as having access to the cloud-based version.

## SPECIALTY SITES

If you don't need the power and complexity of a full-fledged graphical editor in your browser, you could use a specialty application that specializes in just one thing. FotoFlexer, at http://fotoflexer.com, is an excellent choice if you just need to fix up some photos. With this application, you get easy red-eye removal and one-click "auto" settings that make your photographs look better. Another possible specialty application for images—photos or drawings—is LunaPic at http://www.lunapic.com. With LunaPic you get many filters that apply various effects—generally paint or liquid effects—to your images. If you have a photograph that you'd like to make look like a painting, or an image you'd like to make look like it is underwater, you will be

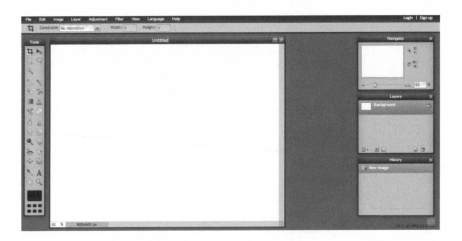

**Figure 11.2.   Pixlr's editing screen.**

able to do so pretty easily with this service. Other effects that give the same sort of look to photos or images are available there as well.

SVG Edit (most current version at this time—http://svg-edit.googlecode. com/svn/branches/2.6/editor/svg-editor.html), found at https://code.google. com/p/svg-edit/, is a bit different than any of the other graphical editors mentioned in this chapter. All of the editors presented so far have been pixel-based (raster) editors. SVG Edit is a vector image editor (though it can handle raster images as well, if you prefer). Instead of painting an image with a set number of pixels, vector images are drawn using points and fills—and are capable of being resized without any loss in quality. The process of saving your image is very different as well. Instead of saving a picture file, svg files are text—you save the text file with an .svg extension and then you can either embed that code using the HTML <embed> or <object> tags or you can copy the text of the .svg file directly into the HTML code. More information on how to use an SVG graphic in your web page can be found at the W3Schools site (http://www.w3schools.com/svg/svg_inhtml.asp). SVG, besides being scalable with no loss of quality, is also scriptable—you can make your image move with the application of some JavaScript. This file format is supported by all modern browsers (with the exception of IE 8) and is a good way to make sure your logo or other images are pretty, no matter how big or small they need to be on your web pages. SVG, being an XML markup language, is a completely different way to create images on the web. The W3Schools (linked above) have a good tutorial on using SVG markup to make graphics do more than just look pretty on your web pages, but if you just want an image without concern for how it will look when expanded or

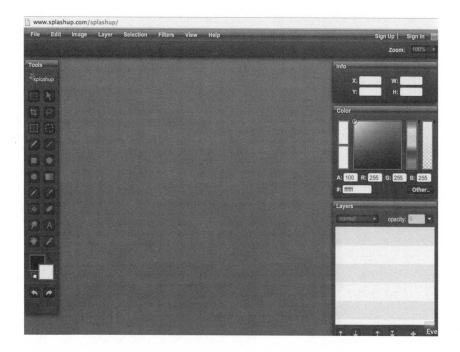

**Figure 11.3. Splashup's editing screen.**

how it can interact with your page, a raster JPEG, GIF, or PNG image will do just as well.

## CLOUD-BASED IMAGE STORAGE

Of course, creating images isn't the only thing you can do in the cloud. Image storage is a natural fit for a cloud-based service. There are many services that will store images for you—many more than can be included in this book. I will make note of two that both are popular and include their own image-editing features. A quick Google search will likely find you many more options if you prefer not to either pay for Flickr's premium features or put more data into Google's Picasa than necessary.

Flickr is one of the first really popular photo-centric sites on the web. There is a free version, but you are limited to seeing only the last two hundred images that you uploaded. Paying $25 a year, however, gets you access to all of your images all of the time. Flickr has within it the Aviary image editor. You can use Flickr's slideshow features to make a slideshow of your images on your website fairly easily, and you can organize your photos

**Figure 11.4. Sumopaint's editing screen.**

into bundles and sets to make them easier to display and show off both on your website and on others.

Picasa is a similar program, though Google owns it. As with Flickr, there is a formerly independent graphical editor (Picnik) included in the service so that you can make quick edits to your images as you upload them. Picasa is now pretty heavily integrated into Google's G+ service, but it is free. With Picasa, you can share and display images, though you don't have quite the range of options that you can get with a Flickr account.

Both Flickr and Picasa include desktop uploaders—little programs that let you easily add pictures to your cloud-based storage site. They also have online uploading options, and Picasa has a G+ uploading option that will take a photo taken by an Android phone with the G+ application on it and automatically upload it to the G+ account that is connected to that phone. The images aren't automatically shared, but they are uploaded almost instantly, making it a nice way to back up images and an easy way to share images immediately, even when you are out of the library at an event.

## USING CLOUD-BASED GRAPHICAL EDITORS AT YOUR LIBRARY

Besides using these tools at events outside the library, there are other ways to use cloud-based graphics editors. As the basis for patron classes, they do double duty in giving your patrons options to the big and expensive, but well-known, editors out there and in letting you provide a classroom's worth of editors at no cost beyond the basic class lab hardware you probably already have. They also provide a way for nonmarketing or nongraphic staff mem-

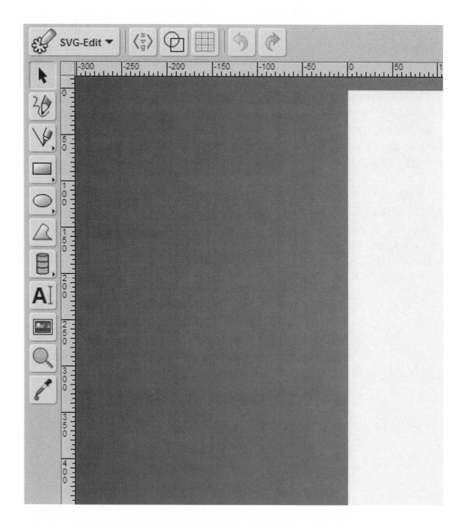

**Figure 11.5. The SVG editor interface.**

bers to contribute their skills to the library without a large software investment. If you have a staff member who is willing to caption and upload pictures to the website while they are working a public desk or even during downtime in their own job, you can let them do that without worrying about licensing and tracking another copy of Photoshop in your library. The ability to make quick edits from a public desk or an outside event or whatever workstation your staff may be using at the moment is a big benefit of these cloud-based services, even before you begin to factor in the price.

Some of the things that you want to look for in a good cloud image editor are the ability to save in multiple formats, the ability to open multiple formats, and a flexible filtering system that gives you a lot of options to touch up photos or alter other graphics you may need to post. Many of the options mentioned in this chapter are mobile-friendly—which makes them very easy to use at remote programs—and all of them are accessible via the browser on a laptop or tablet, again making them easy to use remotely. While your organization may never be able to give up the power and options of a full desktop graphical editor like Photoshop or GIMP, it is nice to know that there are options out there that will let you do quick edits instantly or that will work in a pinch when your more powerful computers are unavailable. There are a multitude of reasons why a library might need to edit an image—from adjusting the colors of a logo to match a branding campaign to taking the red-eye out of a picture of kids having fun at your programs. Being able to quickly adjust an image to suit your needs is completely possible in the cloud without a huge investment of money or hardware.

# Chapter Twelve

# Security

One of the most important points to keep in mind when dealing with cloud services and deciding which services to use—or even whether to use any at all—is security. While there are trade-offs with cloud-based services when it comes to security, just as there are with convenience, price, and features, the lack of security consciousness in the cloud is far more likely to have serious consequences than a lack of features or convenience. Putting your data in the cloud means that you lose some of the "security by obscurity" that many libraries rely on. They are too small with too little valuable data to be really targeted by hackers and crackers—but adding their data to hundreds or thousands of other organizations in a single data storage point can make their data much more attractive to bad guys.

That isn't to say that a cloud-based solution is always more dangerous. If you don't have a top-notch security person on your team at your library, the cloud may well be more secure than your in-house computers. Like most other features, security is scalable and big servers with lots of data can afford to have big security fences and brains around to keep that data safe.

Much of what you decide will depend on your willingness to embrace risk. For some library data—the storage of images, for an example from a recent chapter—the risk of someone "breaking in" to your storage service and "stealing" your data is pretty slight. Those images are open to stealing from the site they are being used on; there is no need to get into your Flickr or Picasa account to steal them. In that case, the risk of a not-secure service is essentially nil. Going back a few chapters, however, to the cloud-based ILS—that is a different story. An ILS stores patron data, data that libraries need to keep very safe. The ILS vendors generally put a great deal of their resources into securing the connection between them and your library, so the data can't be stolen while in transit, and securing their servers as well, so the data can't easily be stolen directly from them. That being said, no solution that involves connected computers is completely risk-proof. Even a locally hosted server in your building that only communicates between floors in your library has risks—the connection itself could be vulnerable to packet sniffer on your wireless network or someone could surreptitiously plug into your wired network and get access to the data that way.

However you decide to go, between cloud-based or locally hosted resources, security should be something everyone—from the director to the maintenance people—think about on a very regular basis. If you go with locally hosted services, they need to be kept behind locked doors and secure from the public. If you go with cloud-based services, contracts need to be scrutinized to ensure that the vendor is security conscious and takes some responsibility for their end of the security responsibilities.

## CLOUD SECURITY BEST PRACTICES

The following best practices are adapted from IT Business Edge (http://www.itbusinessedge.com/slideshows/show.aspx?c=89653&slide=2)    and McAfee (http://blogs.mcafee.com/security-connected/top-15-cloud-security-best-practices):

- Consider security from the outset; don't leave it until the end.
- Make sure your data is portable—if there is a lack of security, you should be able to get your data out and to another provider easily.
- Keep an eye on things; monitor as much as you can.
- Have a plan in case things go wrong and share it.
- Use SECaaS (Security as a Service) options—automatic backups to the cloud, monitoring services in the cloud, etc.
- Start with low-risk services to get your feet wet.
- Include in the contract the ability to audit the vendor's security as needed; the inclusion of your organization in security bulletins and notices; security and service-level agreements (SLAs) that work for you, not just for the vendor.
- Keep your browsers as up to date and as well patched as possible.

In general, keeping safe in the cloud requires the same kind of diligence and forethought as keeping safe in your location. Instead of confirming that your servers are behind locked doors, you confirm that they are covered by an enforceable amount of security. That last point, keeping your browser up to date, is included because you use your browser to access much of what you do in the cloud. Even if your vendor goes to great lengths to secure your data in their data center, if your browser is old and becomes compromised, you will lose data and it will be your fault. You can require all the security in the world from the cloud provider, but if you don't make sure your systems are up to date and well patched, you will be vulnerable.

Another issue to keep in mind when evaluating cloud services is the ability to remove your data in a usable format. If the cloud vendor you choose doesn't have a data export feature that gives you back all of your data in a format that you can use to import it into another service, you will essentially be stuck with that vendor no matter what. Even if they break the contract and fail to provide the security you need, you won't have a good way to change vendors and go with another company. If the vendor goes out of business or just closes down the service you are using, not being able to get your data out could be a disaster as well. Just keep in mind, as you are shopping for a vendor, that data exporting is something that is very important and should be considered before you ever sign up for a service.

## CLOUD PRIVACY

Part of the issue of security in the cloud is privacy in the cloud. Just as we have a duty to keep patron data private, our cloud vendors need to keep our data private, unless we specifically want to share it (in the case of image storage, for example). Using the cloud security software listed below helps to keep your data private—one of the biggest ways that data is leaked is by hackers getting into databases and taking the information. Your state may have requirements that you must meet in keeping patron data private and protected. Check with your state library association or your lawyer to make sure you know what you have to do and what your vendors have to do to ensure patron privacy on networked systems.

Another big data leak point, however, is lost or stolen equipment. The BYOD (Bring Your Own Device) trend that is causing major data issues in corporations is in play in libraries as well. Many times people access patron data using their phone or iPad and don't realize that the data is stored on the device, easily accessible to a thief or to a skilled hacker on a public wireless network. Even if library workers use the library's laptops or other equipment, however, that doesn't mean it too can't be stolen or hacked. Your IT department needs to work out ways to keep your mobile equipment secure and limit the use of personal equipment such as phones or tablets. A blanket prohibition against their use may be counterproductive—people will still use them; they just won't tell your IT department that they are doing it—but keeping some limits on what services employees can access via their equipment is a workable solution that most employees should feel capable of complying with while still being able to do their job.

Another thing you can do to help preserve patron privacy is to work with vendors to help them understand what is important to keep private (patron data, checkout history, etc.). Let them know what is most important for you to keep secure so that they are deploying the majority of their efforts in the right ways. Most vendors will work to keep all of your data secure, but they may be willing to do extra monitoring or more frequent maintenance if they know that the server running your cloud ILS contains very sensitive information.

Finally, after you have done all that work to make the data on your cloud secure, you need to make sure that the data is secure between the cloud and your computer. Most modern browsers come with high-bit encryption (at least 128-bit) available. Generally, you will see a padlock somewhere in the browser's edge (either at the bottom or in the address bar—depending on the browser) that is locked tight when the connection you have with a website is encrypted. The Chrome browser has a good explanation of encryption and how to determine if your connection is encrypted at http://support.google.com/chrome/bin/answer.py?hl=en-GB&answer=95617. Searching through the help on your favorite browser will show you how that browser handles encrypted content and how it displays the fact that the content is encrypted to you. Once you are sure you have an encrypted connection (at the very least make sure you are using https:// as the beginning of the web address to which you are connecting) and you know that your vendor is ensuring that your data is secure on their end, you can be confident that your information is reasonably safe.

## CLOUD SECURITY SOFTWARE (SECaaS)

There are cloud-based versions of traditional security software, too. You can deploy cloud-based firewalls or antivirus programs in the same way you can deploy them traditionally, for the most part. The big concerns with cloud-based security are maintenance and timeliness. If your antivirus service only updates once a month, it's essentially useless to you. If your cloud firewall doesn't get patched and updated on a regular basis, it too is vulnerable and useless. Having firm commitments from your vendor about the amount of updating/patching they do and the frequency for which updates and patches are checked is very important. There are many examples of both cloud firewalls and cloud antivirus software—below are just two, but, as always, a quick search will find many more that might suit your organization just as well.

CloudProxy (http://cloudproxy.sucuri.net/) is one example of a web-based firewall. It protects websites and web applications from various types of threats, including DoS (Denial of Service) attacks and many others. At this time there is no free version; pricing starts at $9.99 a month and that includes monitoring by their "security operations center." If you are hosting your website or application somewhere that has less than ideal security, this is a way to beef that up and keep the bad guys from getting into your site.

Panda Cloud Antivirus (http://www.cloudantivirus.com) has both Free and Pro versions of its cloud-based antivirus. This is a bit different than most cloud-based services because there is a program that lives on your computer—antivirus won't really work without something being present on your machine—but the program is managed and updated through the cloud without any need for your intervention at all. With traditional antivirus, you sometimes have to click "yes" to get updates or upgrades for the program. Panda Cloud Antivirus updates "in the cloud"; then all the connected clients get updated shortly thereafter. For machines that are primarily used by the public, this is a good way to get updates without requiring your patrons to approve the update or upgrade themselves. It is set-it-and-forget-it antivirus, which makes it more secure than antivirus that might require more interaction from you—especially if you don't have dedicated IT staff to deal with these kinds of things.

## BLAKE CARVER, LIBRARY SECURITY SPECIALIST

Blake Carver (http://eblake.com/resume/), owner and operator of the LIS-Host and LISNews websites, as well as several others, is a frequent speaker on the library conference circuit. He specializes in online security and is the go-to guy when libraries have questions or concerns about securing their online presence. I asked him a couple of questions while I was gathering information for this chapter and have his answers below.

R: So, Blake, can you share one thing that you think is most important, security-wise, for libraries to consider when they are looking at cloud-based services?

B: I don't know if there's *one* thing, but it's important to do your homework if you're not going with a major provider (e.g., Amazon). In general I think people are moving stuff to the cloud to save money/time. All the cloud stuff makes scaling up services *so* easy, and it's generally less expensive. The problem (security-wise) is of course you have no choice but to trust they (the cloud people) are doing things right. There's no way to *really* know if they have things locked down. So I think one major thing is to just do your homework. Ask them questions about how they handle security. Maybe you won't understand the answers, but the important thing is they have answers.

R: Do you have any good security resources that are usable by nontechnical experts?

B: For someone *really* dedicated to it: https://www.sans.org/course/cloud-security-fundamentals. SANS in general has great resources: https://www.sans.org/reading_room/whitepapers/cloud/.

R: So, to finish up the chapter—do you have any good horror stories of libraries who have been burned because of trusting a cloud service?

B: Nope. Luckily. :-)

The major points to look for in a cloud vendor are a willingness to let you monitor your data as much as you need, a clear and understandable SLA that includes security measures, and encrypted connections to your data. Review the best practices in cloud security before you sign any contract with any vendor and be sure that the vendor understands exactly what is most important for you to keep safe. Keeping all of this in mind and, as Blake said, doing your homework to make sure your vendor is as security conscious as you—if not more—will do a lot toward keeping your patron's data and your library's information safe from prying eyes.

Remember that unless you are employing a team of security experts, keeping your data in-house is not necessarily any safer than putting it in the cloud. You need to determine the amount of risk you are willing to accept, determine which solution provides no more risk than what you are willing to accept, and go with the one that meets your needs. There may be times you choose not to use a cloud service because none of the vendors can assure you of their security bona fides. That just means that you may have to table the idea for a year or two and then try again; there are always new services and new vendors coming into the cloud arena. Stay patient and one will likely come along that you can work with.

# Chapter Thirteen

# Training

Along with e-mail, training in the cloud is likely the most common thing libraries do in the cloud. Any webinar or e-class that you take via the web is, in general, cloud-based training. That being said, this chapter will be a rundown of the various places you can go, in the cloud and without leaving your desk, for learning opportunities in libraries. Cloud-based training is, at the time of this writing, really taking off with MOOCs (massive open online courses), webinars, Moodle-based classes, and many other strangely named learning opportunities popping up everywhere you look. There are many classes, tutorials, demos, and other forms of learning that can be had online with many different training types for different types of learners. This chapter will focus on the training that can be accessed online, through the Internet—without an in-person component. Both synchronous (at the same time) and asynchronous (at different times) training will be presented.

Synchronous training involves everyone gathering in the same place at the same time. With the advent of the Internet and cloud-based communications, the place can now be virtual as well as physical. With physical synchronous classes, everyone gets together in a classroom or training lab and learns at the same time in the same place. With virtual synchronous training, everyone logs into the same virtual space—a Collaborate webinar "room" or a Google Hangout or even an IRC (Internet Relay Chat) channel—at the same time to attend training together while in different physical spaces.

Asynchronous training happens at different times, but in the same virtual place. Many virtual classrooms using software like Moodle (http://www.moodle.org) or Blackboard (http://www.blackboard.com) are asynchronous in that they let students log on anytime to read or watch the lesson, read and contribute to the discussion boards, and upload assignments whenever they have the time to do so. Of course, time limits are generally imposed for discussions and assignments, but within those time constraints (say, during the course of a week you must read or watch the provided lesson, make two comments on a discussion board, and upload a written assignment) the student can do these required tasks at any time. This is an excellent way to make use of training from all over the world; if you can access the lessons at any time, it doesn't matter when the teacher's "day" is—everything can be done according to your time zone.

Between those two types of training are numerous ways to get information from an expert in the subject to your staff. Professional development depends on learning new skills and understanding new ways of doing things, so training is vital to modern workers in any industry, but especially in knowledge-based industries like librarianship. Staying relevant and keeping current are both vital activities for all library staff.

## TRAINING SOFTWARE

There are many different platforms from which training can be offered. E-courses like the ones profiled in the next section use different kinds of software to facilitate the classes. Moodle, the open-source class software, is one of the most popular platforms for noneducational institutions to use. It's free, easy to set up, and extremely configurable. You can get a quick look at how students can make use of Moodle at http://docs.moodle.org—there are a number of tutorials available that can give you a taste of what taking a class using Moodle would be like. Both ALA and Library Juice Academy (more about those training sources later) use the Moodle platform for their e-courses.

For established educational institutions such as colleges, you may be taking an online course using the Blackboard platform. This is the "industry-standard" platform that many educational institutions use. You can get an idea of what classes are like using the Blackboard software at http://www.blackboard.com/quicktutorials/quicktutorials.htm. Since the Blackboard software is not free or open source, you will generally only encounter it in more expensive classes or if you are getting your degree online.

## WEBINARS

Another kind of software you will be exposed to in the course of doing training online is webinar platforms. From GoToWebinar to Collaborate (now owned by Blackboard) to Adobe Connect, you will likely encounter a number of different platforms offering a huge variety of classes. They all generally work in the same way, allowing an instructor and perhaps a host to have full audio and visual control of a "room" in the webinar platform. They can upload slides or videos or use whiteboard or screen-sharing features that are common to most webinar software. The students can either connect via phone or through a headset connected to their computer and, depending on the class and the number of participants, may be able to access the audio to speak in the webinar as well. For larger classes, this would be chaotic, so they usually limit participants to hearing, seeing, and chatting, not speaking, in the class. The host or other facilitator can follow the chats and ask the instructor the questions that come up during the class. While Moodle- and Blackboard-based classes can be asynchronous, webinars are almost always synchronous—they are scheduled for a specific time and everyone is expected to be present during the webinar. Many are archived and those archives are an excellent way to get information, but they aren't interactive and questions won't be answered unless your question came up during the class and was asked by one of the people who attended the actual synchronous class. Archives are valuable, however, as training tools in themselves as they are excellent ways to refresh staff's knowledge and a way to let some students rewatch the class in order to fully grasp the material.

## MOOCs

MOOCs (massive open online courses) are a fairly new entry to Internet-based learning. They provide a way for a lot (up to fifty thousand in some cases) of students to access a class that is being offered by, usually, an institute of higher education. Coursera (http://www.coursera.org), Udacity (http://www.udacity.com), and edX (http://www.edx.org) are three of the bigger MOOC providers. They feature college-level classes taught by college professors using the same materials as are used in their physical classes at their college. Everything from physics to sociology to game theory is offered. At the time of this writing, Coursera was offering 338 courses from 62 different universities. Those classes are all offered for free, though if you want actual college credit for any of them (and that is only available for some classes at some MOOCs), there is a cost involved. Many others offer a certificate of completion for a small fee, even if they don't offer college credits. In the fall of 2013, the first library-school-related MOOC will be offered through San Jose State University—the Hyperlinked Library (http://slisweb.sjsu.edu/programs/moocs/hyperlinked-library-mooc). Many of the other classes offered through the other MOOC platforms would be extremely helpful for library staff, too.

## LESS POPULATED E-COURSES

Between the ALA brand e-courses and the Library Juice Academy e-courses, you have a number of choices for classes on library-related topics with a much smaller class size. Both platforms offer more intimate learning experiences with approximately twenty or so students for the average class. Library Juice Academy offers a few classes a month for, mostly, under $200 per course. Each of them does offer CEUs (continuing education units) for library staff who need to have those in order to fulfill job requirements, and the courses are all taught by library-land instructors. ALA's e-learning store is similar—library-related workshops, webinars, and e-courses for various topics at various times. I have taught courses for each of those platforms—project management for Library Juice and Google Docs with Maurice Coleman for ALA e-courses. They are very similar platforms, though ALA has been around longer and has more selection in class types.

At the time of this writing, some of the classes being offered at the ALA e-learning store were:

• Linked In for Librarians (a workshop);
• Handy Tech Tools for Library Outreach (a workshop);
• Teaching Information Literacy to College Students (an e-course/e-book bundle);
• Copyright for Teachers and Librarians (an e-course/e-book bundle); and
• How to Be a Webinar Superstar (webinar).

The classes being offered at Library Juice Academy included:

• Cataloging for the Non-Cataloger;
• The Mechanics of Metadata;
• Introduction to the Semantic Web;
• Copyright 101 for Librarians;
• Embedded Librarianship;
• Certificate in UX (User Experience)—(a series of classes); and
• Webinar Series with Everylibrary: Libraries on the Ballot (webinars).

Classes change regularly, so those classes may not be offered now—but new classes are being offered all the time and, at least at the ALA store, you can buy access to archived webinars. Both organizations take requests, too—so if there is a topic you particularly want to learn about and you can arrange a minimum number of students, they may be able to create content on request.

Whichever one you choose, they are pretty affordable ways to get particular staff up to speed on a topic with a workshop or to provide an hour's training to many different staff members through a webinar or to get an in-depth look at a particular topic through an e-course. They are also both focused on library-related topics so even for a topic like project management, which isn't library specific, the class is tailored for library staff using library-related examples and gives library-specific solutions to issues the students may have. Other platforms, however, may spring up at any time, so be sure to pay attention to your library mailing lists, social networks, and other resources to find out about new classes offered by new organizations.

## TRAINING RESOURCES

Social networks and library mailing lists are both excellent ways to learn about new classes being offered, but they aren't the only ways to find out what's out there. Many library-related organizations—from state libraries to library associations—offer "roundups" of upcoming training opportunities. Other options for finding training are trainers' organizations in both local and national library associations. They generally have some sort of training calendar that they maintain that you can use to see what training sessions are coming up. Other places to get information on training are the sections within your professional organization—ALA or SLA, for example—that provide support for both library-land trainers and for people looking for library-specific training.

## CONTINUING EDUCATION ROUNDUPS

Both state libraries I've worked with—Missouri and Kansas—have had some sort of continuing education (CE) "roundup" or calendar that pulls the various training opportunities both in-state and nationally together into one place. Your state library may do the same thing. A quick check of neighboring states shows the Nebraska Library Commission provides a training calendar (http://nlc.nebraska.gov/calendar/) that is very similar to Missouri's training calendar. Other organizations also offer roundups of CE opportunities like Kansas's. One such roundup is the RLACE (Reference Librarians Association CE) roundup they post on their blog. April of 2013's entry can be found at http://rlace.info/2013/04/01/ce-around-the-state-april-edition-2/. Your state or association probably has an organizational CE calendar that they use to find and advertise educational opportunities that are relevant to their members. If your library has a trainer on staff, be sure to check with them frequently for training opportunities outside of the library—they may have a great resource for finding new sources of training for you and your staff.

## LEARNRT FROM ALA

At http://www.ala.org/learnrt/node/19, the ALA's LearnRT (Learning Round Table) focuses on training and trainers in libraries. While the focus of the LearnRT is more for trainers, they also do a great job of advertising training opportunities for librarians. If you are having difficulties finding training for your organization that covers a particular topic, you can sometimes find a trainer associated with the LearnRT group who knows libraries and library issues and is affordable as well. The group can put you in touch with someone who can work with you if you just can't find anything already offered.

With shrinking budgets and quickly changing landscapes, finding training that is both affordable and relevant can be tricky. Affordability of training is helped by taking advantage of online sources of training—using the cloud to provide a learning environment for your staff that works for everyone. Just because the training is online, though, doesn't mean that it's always going to be asynchronous with no chance to ask an instructor specific questions—many cloud-based classes now use cloud-based tools like Google Hangouts to provide in-person office hours for their classes, giving students a chance to interact with the teacher and ask questions in real time. Between the availability of real-time conversation and time-shifted forums, cloud-based training can be tailored to fit just about any organization's need for keeping staff up to date.

When you look for online training, try to find training—and trainers—relevant to the particular issues that crop up around nonprofit organizations like libraries. Look for classes or courses that incorporate both synchronous and asynchronous elements so that all students can communicate as they prefer, and try to find classes that offer some sort of credit or at least certificate of completion so that your staff can keep track of their learning and prove that they are getting the professional development that is needed in today's rapidly changing environments. I deliberately left off vendor-based training in this chapter because while it can be very useful for limited applications, for most folks, general training providers like ALA or Library Juice will be more broadly useful and have more widely needed topics.

## Chapter Fourteen

# Afterword

The cloud can be an amazing place—full of free and inexpensive services and tools for you to use in your library. The lure of "free" can be very tempting, too, but there are things to consider before you jump on these services. Beyond the security issues—which are really no more severe than for locally hosted services—and the pricing issues—which are usually less than locally hosted services due to the economies of scale that cloud vendors can provide—there are other things to consider.

Each service featured in this book, from the cloud-based ILS to the online training options available today, has its pros and cons. Being able to understand what those pros and cons might be and being able to evaluate your options in a clearheaded way will increase your chances of a successful cloud-services venture. The cloud, by its very nature, encourages seat-of-the-pants decisions and full-steam-ahead risk taking. Signing up for a new service is so easy, and so affordable and everybody else is doing it. . . . What you need to arm yourself with when you venture into making decisions about cloud services are clear goals for each service, an understanding of what is and isn't possible for each service, and a willingness to test and experiment. Hopefully, what you have learned about various cloud services in this book will equip you to make smart decisions in the future. The rest of this chapter includes more tools for you to use both in and alongside the cloud.

First I've included a checklist for cloud vendors. Make a copy of this page (make several!) or download a copy from this book's website and use it every time you venture into the cloud to try a new service. After a while, you'll instinctively look for these things, but at first, it helps to have a little reminder of what you need to look for in your cloud vendor.

Next is a list of desktop image editors that won't break the bank. While browser-based image editing—as described in chapter 11—is very helpful for quick edits while you are out, having a full-fledged graphic editor on a computer in your library gives you more ability to produce images and photographs that look just the way you want. I've included both raster (pixel-based) and vector (line-based) image editors that are both free and open source on that page. These editors I've included have been around for many years and will likely be around for many more. Since they are free, feel free to download all of them and use the one that works the best for you—and that you work the best in.

Finally, there is a list of readings and resources for security in the cloud. Securing our data and ensuring that our patron's data is private are both incredibly important parts of the librarian's job. The resources given here will be a good start, but things change very, very quickly in the online world, and the mailing lists and other collaborative spaces where people can go to check on new issues and find out about recent events are just as, if not more, important as having a strong grounding in security concepts. If you get nothing else from this book, read the security chapter (chapter 12), look at some of Blake Carver's presentations (and go see him in person if you can), and make use of the security resources provided for you in this chapter.

The cloud changes constantly, as do real-life in-the-sky clouds, and staying a step ahead of the curve is difficult. Knowing the basics of how things work in the cloud, though, will help. I hope this book gives you those basics and that you are able to make good decisions about cloud-based services using some of the resources and ideas here.

The following pages include a checklist for you to use whenever you start to evaluate a cloud service—not every service will require all the features that this checklist mentions, but it will give you a good place to start asking questions. After that is a list of the currently available free and open-source desktop graphical editors—most mentioned in chapter 11—that you can use to supplement your cloud-based editors without paying a huge price in licensing fees. Finally, the last resource includes a list of reading material for the library interested in keeping their data and their patrons' data secure against hackers. It is by no means authoritative, but it is a good start, and it includes some mailing lists that I have found useful when I have security-related questions myself.

## CHECKLIST FOR CLOUD VENDORS

1. Uptime guarantees—how many 9's will they promise and what will they give you if they don't meet those promises?

2. What kind of service-level agreement (SLA) do they provide?

3. Upgrade/patching schedule—do they stay current with the software or are they always a version or two behind?

4. What is their security plan? Can you get a copy?

5. What certifications (security) do they hold?

6. Are there monitoring (network, security, SLA compliance) tools already in place? Will they make them available to you?

7. Can you speak to current customers or users?

8. Will they give you a fairly generous demonstration period?

9. Will you get a specific representative or support person for your organization?

10. How long have they been in business?

11. What kind of "chatter" is happening about them on social networking sites? (Lots of complaints on Twitter? Nothing but really happy customers on Facebook?)

## FREE/OPEN-SOURCE DESKTOP GRAPHICAL EDITORS

GIMP 2.0 (http://www.gimp.org)
Gimpshop (http://www.gimpshop.org)
Inkscape (http://www.inkscape.org, vector graphics)
Paint.net (for Windows only, not open source, http://www.getpaint.net/
index.html)

## SECURITY READING

Amazon's Best Practices for Security Whitepaper: http://media.
amazonwebservices.com/Whitepaper_Security_Best_Practices_2010.
pdf
Introduction to Securing a Cloud Environment (SANS): https://www.
sans.org/reading_room/whitepapers/cloud/introduction-securing-
cloud-environment_34052
Following Incidents into the Cloud (SANS): https://www.sans.org/
reading_room/whitepapers/cloud/incidents-cloud_33619
Best Browser Extensions That Protect Your Privacy: http://lifehacker.
com/the-best-browser-extensions-that-protect-your-privacy-
479408034

## MAILING LISTS

SEC4LIB—http://sec4lib.wordpress.com/about/
Security Basics List—http://seclists.org/basics/
Wordpress Security Alerts—http://www.wordfence.com/subscribe-to-
the-wordfence-email-list/
Drupal Security Alerts—http://drupal.org/security

# Index

# About the Author

**Robin Hastings** is the director of technology services at the Northeast Kansas Library System in Lawrence, Kansas. In that capacity, she consults with librarians in the northeast part of the state about technology in their libraries and manages a technical support staff and a system administrator who help their libraries achieve their technology goals. She can also be found presenting about all the cool things her library does at various conferences around the world. She has presented on Mashups, Cloud Computing, RSS, Drupal, Library Learning 2.0, project management, and many other topics.

She is the author of *Collaboration 2.0 Library Technology Report* and *Microblogging and Lifestreaming in Libraries*, as well as several articles in library-related journals.